Andy
I wish you
Health, Happiness
&
Peace!

*[signature]*

1

# What people are saying about "I'm Still Here"

"Kevin Irish's Book 'I'm Still Here -A Cancer Survivor's Story' is a truly inspiring story of a man's will to live despite his diagnosis of cancer.
It makes you stop and think about life and how you deal with the curve balls that are thrown at you. It reminded me of that saying, "The true test of character isn't how you are on your *best* days, it's how you are on your *worst* days...or when things don't go right".
I, personally, never had a *clue* to the day-to-day process of chemo/radiation therapy, not to mention the thoughts that can run through a person's mind. The recounting of his emotional responses and physical reactions to his cancer and chemotherapy are alternately hilarious and terrifying, and I found myself feeling deep empathy with him.
It takes a special person to want to make others happy even while going through the rigors of chemo/radiation and that is exactly what Kevin does throughout his arduous battle with cancer. This book is a *must read* just to give a perspective on facing problems in life head-on with a positive, can-do attitude laced with humor. I never thought that I would laugh at anything even *remotely* related to cancer, but thanks to Kevin, I did, and I take my hat off to everyone and anyone who has had to watch/care for a friend or loved one battling cancer and especially for those brave people who have *beaten this disease*!"

**Theresa Seymour, Insurance Agent**

---

"Kevin Irish has been through it. Condemned by cancer, and then redeemed by a combination of traditional and mainstream slash and burn treatment, then backed up by methods and therapies that big pharma and big medicine don't officially endorse, Kevin is--as befits the title of this book--"still here." Stick around and let his story sink into you. And if you or one you love has to face this all too prevalent disease, take practical and spiritual hope that you too will prevail."

**-Tom Stevens, Writer, Producer and Creative Director**

---

"This book is a poignant, detailed account of one man's journey with cancer. Kevin's brutal honesty is refreshing as he recounts his struggles and triumphs with the disease and treatments. It's sure to ignite a wide range of emotions in the reader, especially in the ones facing the same devastating diagnosis and treatment.
Kevin's remarkable recovery is due, in part, to his *sheer will* and *determination* to live, and to the dedicated people in cancer research. Let's continue to band together and pray for those currently in the fight."

**-Rosa Streng, Salon Proprietor**

"When I started reading I'M STILL HERE, I found it hard to stop as it is very well written and truly keeps you interested. Kevin is very open and honest about the emotional roller coaster and fear he experienced after getting his cancer diagnosis.

Through his strength and positive attitude during his cancer treatment, Kevin shows us it is possible to handle more than we ever imagined we could handle. This book gives hope to others who are facing a cancer diagnosis and helps their loved ones to understand."

-Linda Clark-Thayer, Retired

---

"Kevin, thank you for sharing your amazing story! It made me sad, then, at times you made me laugh! It's so very rare to find humor and such open honesty and positive reactions and feelings...when going through this horrible disease. Kevin's story I'M STILL HERE was gifted to me by Kevin himself and his story has been my inspiration as I am sure it has and will be to those who read this amazing book!

Kevin is an amazing man, a true inspiration to all of us who have been touched by cancer. People look for miracles, sometimes you have to be the miracle...I think Kevin is just that!"

-Carole Young, Cancer Patient/SURVIVOR

---

There's one word I have to say, "WOW!" This is one of the most inspiring books ever! "I'M STILL HERE" has definitely changed my perspective of cancer.

I knew that cancer was bad, but I never knew what happened to people who have cancer and I didn't even know what "chemotherapy" was until I read this.

I can't believe this all happened to you. Even with all of the horrible treatments and chemo, you stayed positive, literally through *everything*...and *still* helped others facing the same things you were! That is such a gift for a person to stay positive throughout that.

This book gets an "A+++"!!! It is so detailed that now, I can relate a little bit how to help my cousin who has breast cancer. Now I know how I can help her because I understand what she is going through. I was sympathetic and happy when I read this book!

I recommend this book to everyone, especially cancer patients to help them stay positive with a truly inspiring book! One of my favorites!

-Cayla Byron 1 2, Student

(My golf buddy's daughter)

# I'm Still Here - A Cancer Survivors Story

Copyright ©2012
Infinity 510² Partners
Kevin K Irish

Written and Illustrated by Kevin K Irish
Edited by Kevin K Irish
Assisting Editors, Tom and Nancy Stevens
The front and back cover created and designed by Kevin K Irish

(The Author may be contacted thru his charity e-mail)
kevskause@hotmail.com

## Notice of Rights

All rights reserved. No portion of this book may be, stored in a retrieval system, or transmitted in any form or by any means electronic, mechanical, photocopying, or otherwise, except by the inclusion of brief quotations in a review to be printed or published on the web, without permission from the author and the publisher.

This book is "non-fiction" and a detailed account of real events.
The names of individuals mentioned in this book have been omitted to protect their privacy.

Printed and bound in the USA
ISBN 0-9788065-6-5 (ISBN 10)
ISBN 978-0-9788065-6-9 (ISBN 13)

10 9 8 7 6 5 4 3 2

## A Cancer Survivors Story

### Written and Illustrated by Kevin K Irish

# I'm Still Here

This book is dedicated to all
cancer patients, survivors,
families and loved ones...

...past, present and future...

**...and to that *final cancer patient*.**

# Preface

My name is Kevin K Irish and as of the writing of this book, I am a 3 ½ year stage IIIA lung cancer survivor... this is my story.

I was a Senior Design Engineer in the automotive field for over 23 years (retired); I am an established artist, published author and amateur historian/philosopher. I am also an *avid* golfer, cat lover (*all* animals actually...I just *really* like *cats*!) I have been divorced for over six years and I have no children (except for my step son, who is still in my life and I love him dearly)... and for the last six years I have been single, enjoying life and living in St. Clair Shores, Michigan with my two cats Sweetie and Puddin. *Prior to my diagnosis*, I would go out to visit my parents and brother a couple times a week (or more when needed) and cook them a nice "home cooked meal" (since mom was 'bed ridden' and my dad and brother don't cook...I just didn't like them eating "carry out" and "nuke-n-puke-microwave" meals!), and took care of whatever they needed done at their home. My mom and dad are both senior citizens and my brother lives with them and helps take care of them. However, after January 24, 2009 I was unable to go out there at all...for obvious reasons.

This book will detail my cancer treatment and what I was feeling; how I was able to cope with it. As every cancer diagnosis and treatment is *different*, I hope by sharing my story, it will show that hope, courage, strength and resolve *really are within us all*. A strong *positive attitude* and *the belief in hope* will get you through your darkest hour, lift you up and give you the *strength* to <u>overcome</u> life's obstacles. I *truly* live life and *appreciate* the *good* life has to offer!

There's an excellent quote from one of my favorite movies which states, "hope is a good thing, perhaps the best of things." I like to say "*Believe* in yourself, stay true to *yourself* and *believe in the ones you love*."

I wish you health, happiness, peace and love.

# Introduction

This was written to encourage current cancer patients...and to help survivors know they were never alone...

*...and to help those who never had cancer to better understand.*

I have talked to so many patients and survivors and as each patient/survivor's circumstances vary from person to person and diagnosis to diagnosis, the one thing in common with all cases is the _fear_.

By writing this book is my intent and desire to offer *understanding* and *compassion* to those who are going through cancer treatments and comfort in understanding for those who are not.

As there are many people involved with the story, friends, families, loved ones and doctors (and total strangers too) I wish to protect their privacy by not using their names in this story. The people, who are mentioned within, will *know* who they are and how they are *so very much appreciated!*

Whether you are currently a cancer patient, a cancer survivor, a family member or friend, someone who is never had cancer, it is my *sincere* hope that what you take away from reading this book will be encouraging and perhaps inspirational to you or those you love, and to provide truth, knowledge, understanding to everyone whose life has been forever changed by cancer entering into their lives. This story is being told *not* for *sympathy*, rather, so others can *understand*!

In these chapters, I will do the best that I can to try to relate to you what my battle with cancer was like and how I was feeling, how I coped with and learned to live a better life *after* cancer.

# Chapters

"Miracles are what seem
impossible...

...*but happen anyway!*"

# Chapter 1

# Before The Storm

I'm going to start this story, if I may, by telling you how I got started and fascinated by the game of golf. One could say that the game of golf *may* have been instrumental in *saving* my life... or at least giving me some *hints* of what lays ahead in my life.

In the spring of 2008 a friend of mine wanted to get me into golfing. He offered to sell me a set of clubs, driver and putter included with the golf bag at a reasonable price and kept bugging me and encouraging me (and *bugging* me...) to give it a try. So, I agreed and he immediately proceeded to have us go to a driving range so I can test out the clubs and he can give me an idea of actually how to swing them.

Once at the driving range, large bucket of balls purchased, we proceeded to go the range. It was intimidating only for the fact that there were others right around me, that where hitting like pros. Obviously they've been playing for a while, then my friend proceeded to set up the ball and show me how to get a basic stance and told me basically want to do, how to swing, where I should keep my eyes focused, how I should twist... the whole 9 yards! So after about 40 to 50 "range balls", my friend decided that I've had enough practice and should go do some actual golfing!

I followed him to a par 3, 9-hole golf course, my friend told me to "grip it and rip it"...which I did. The club followed smoothly to the ball and CRACK! I had made a clean hit and a nice drive that went out onto the fairway pretty well. OMG!! My second shot went too far left and bounced on a green side berm of grass and bounced *right* onto the edge of the green and rolled to about 3 feet short of the hole. Which, by complete and utter luck, I was able to *reach a par 4 hole in 2* which is quite the accomplishment, considering I've never played golf in my life! So, with my trusty new sidekick, my new putter in hand, I proceeded to set up, study the line and putt... and the ball rolled straight into the hole...MY FIRST *BIRDIE*! ☺

And sheer blind LUCK was the ONLY way that was going to happen! ☺

Needless to say, my friend was a bit *perturbed* with me as he proceeded to bogey that first hole. However, the remaining 8 holes were a complete and dismal disappointment. My friend played pretty well and even birdied the 7th hole himself. The bad news is that I shot a 78 on a par 31-9 hole golf course. The good news, of course, is that I had a *blast* doing it! That was it... I was *hooked*! ☺

So it went, for the remaining spring, summer and fall 2008 golf season, I was going to get as much of it as I could and learn as much of it as I could. We played mainly par 3-9 hole "executive" golf courses. Frustrating as it was, most the time, it was still a riot just being outside getting some exercise having fun with a friend. Until September 2008, that's when my golf game was held up because of a kidney stone attack. Not just a *mild* little kidney stone, mind you, but a full-blown OMG called 911, got to get to the hospital quick kind of kidney stone!

*As I'm sure anyone who has had a kidney stone in the past can tell you, it isn't much fun and I will spare you the details.*

I woke up on the morning of September 18 to an excruciating and sharp pain in my stomach and having an uncontrollable urge to throw up. In pain, trying to throw up and sweating profusely I *knew something was wrong.* It was clearly time to call 911!

When the EMTs arrived, they opened my front door and said loudly "Is anybody home? Does anybody need help?"

I called out to them, doubled up on the floor in the bathroom and they immediately came in to help. I was *so* embarrassed to be seen in the state that I was in. They checked me out *quite thoroughly* and quite quickly actually, and then hurried me out to the waiting gurney that was on my front porch and strapped me in, then loaded me into the ambulance. While I was waiting for the ambulance to take me into the hospital, one of the senior citizens that I look after on my street, came over to inquire as to what was going on. At this point the pain is unbearable and I could hear my neighbor questioning the driver of the ambulance from outside the ambulance in the middle of the street, giving the driver 50 questions as to what's going on. This was not unusual for him, he is a wonderful guy, but he's a real chatterbox! At this point

I simply pleaded with the driver and the EMT that we should go to the hospital and I instructed them to tell my neighbor that I will call him as soon as I am able to. I was then rushed to the hospital lights and sirens blasting and before I know it I was wheeled into an ER and had numerous people buzzing around poking and prodding and checking and inspecting me... whisking me away for x-rays and further tests, after all of this commotion, I soon found myself in the emergency room on a gurney waiting for results.

At some point I looked over in the doorway of the room I was in, and there was my own family doctor standing there big as day! He looks surprised and asked me "what the heck are you doing here?" I gave a brief description of the symptoms that had brought me into the emergency room. He quickly pointed out that it sounds like a kidney stone and that I was in good hands and he would make sure that the attending physicians knew that I was *his* patient and that I will be well cared for. Everyone assured me that I was going to be fine... but whatever they were going to do to help me, they haven't done yet! Not long after my doctor left, the attending physician came in the room and told me that I indeed had a kidney stone and that it will pass and then informed me of the procedure that I'm to follow immediately after discharge from the hospital. Simple enough.

On a side note here…while in the hospital, I was also given a full chest x-ray…which by chance SHOWED I had a LARGE tumor on my left lung…yet NO ONE at the hospital informed me of this the whole time I was there! REALLY?

After a few hours I was released from the hospital and given a "clean bill of health". But, since I was taken to the hospital, in an emergency situation, I found myself on the outside of the hospital in an old flannel shirt and a pair of old sweatpants. No socks, no shoes, no wallet, no money… no *car* and no way home! Since it was only about a mile and a half to my home, I decided I'd walk home. Later that day, my golfing buddy called and asked if I would like to go golfing? Of course I would! ☺

We went to the usual "executive" golf course that we have been playing at, and it is at that point, during that round of golf, I started to begin to feel pain between my shoulder blade and my spine in my upper back. I simply *presumed* that I had pulled muscles a little bit or I was aggravating the osteoarthritis in my shoulder. Either way I started to become concerned.

I scheduled an appointment with my own family doctor and was able to get me in within a day or two. Once at my doctors, he did his usual thorough examination didn't see any problems, and suggested that yes indeed I may have just "over did it" while golfing. He referred me to an orthopedic surgeon to get his opinion on the condition. The visit to *this* Doctor, shall we say, wasn't the most pleasant experience I've had visiting a doctor. He was actually *quite* rude and very cold with his approach to the complaint I had. I'd explain that I have a history of arthritis in the shoulder and could he tell me what he thinks; I'm here for a second opinion. He ordered x-rays and upon his report from the x-rays he stated that I had "rotator cuff issues" and recommended I take ibuprofen and ice packs to manage the pain. And I don't think he noticed, nor did he mention, anything *other* than *his* diagnosis.

*The pain wasn't going away... No matter what I tried.*

A couple months later, after golf season had ended, the pain was still persisting and getting more severe. I had noticed a slight, intermittent "spasm" or "twitch" in my left thumb. I didn't think much of it because it wasn't chronic and it wasn't irritating. I continued with ice packs and no golfing to see if this would alleviate the pain and give myself a rest from golfing for little bit. So as the weather turns colder and too cold for golf, I decided not to even attempt to go to the driving range until my shoulder and back felt better.

During this time I kept thinking about someone I used to know many years ago, that had passed away from cancer a few short years earlier. Family members had contacted me to inform me of this person's passing. They described the initial symptoms they had... and told me that this person decided not to do anything. At this point, I was thinking about the whole situation and the shared symptoms.

I was thinking that since I didn't have as *many* symptoms and not as *severe* of symptoms, that I should be okay.

*That was, until January 24, 2009.*

# Chapter 2

# Signs of Trouble Ahead

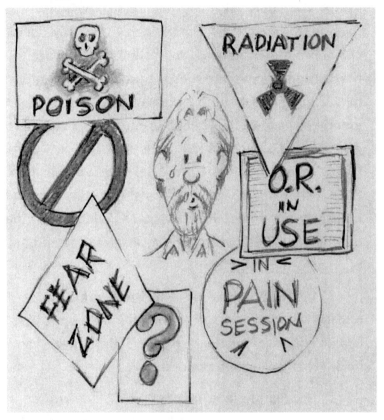

On January 24, 2009 I noticed my left eyelid appeared to be "drooping" and I dismissed it as just my being tired or fatigued. When I had noticed that it was *only* on the left side and the right eyelid still quite normal, that's when I decided to call my doctor and see if he would take me in on an "emergency" basis and briefly described why I was coming in and why I thought it was urgent, they were able to get me in and see me the same day.

Once I was at my doctors, and in an exam room having my vitals taken by the nurse, my mind was filled with thoughts of "what's going on?" My doctor came into the exam room and he immediately noticed the "droop" of my left eyelid. I proceeded to inform him that the eye droop was *why* I requested an emergency exam. He listened to my lungs, listened to my heart and checked my vitals that had just been taken. I was sitting down on the edge of the exam table when he looked me straight in the eye and informed me that I had "Horner's Syndrome" (the drooping eye lid) and that it was a *serious* symptom... of *advanced lung cancer*.

I immediately went completely numb. I looked him in the eye, but I couldn't utter a sound. I just couldn't think of anything to say... I didn't even know what I was feeling at that point...

He told me to remember what I had written in my first book ("Take Another Look... A Guide for Understanding Ourselves") which is my first book about how there's more positive in life the negative; that there is more *good* in life than *bad*.

He then opened up his tablet PC and wanted me to watch a video of a cancer patient with "end-stage" liver cancer. In the video this man was giving an inspirational and motivational seminar. In it, he spoke of the power of *positive thinking* and how it affects and enhances your life. As I watched, my doctor left the exam room and within minutes of him leaving one of the nurses came in the exam room with tears in her eyes and at this point I too was crying.

I have known the doctors and nurses at my doctor's office so well, as I have been going there for over 13 years. She told me that the rest of the staff were all in shock. She told me to stay strong and she informed me that my doctor had given them all directive that whenever I call for any reason, they were to do anything they can to help me out and that he is going to give me his private number when I leave the office (THIS is scaring the *hell* out of me! My Doctor's *private* number?) When my doctor returned, told me he had called the hospital and alerted them that I was coming in IMMEDIATELY for a chest MRI. He told me that he has submitted the orders for the MRI...STAT... and that the hospital is to call him *immediately* with the results. He excused himself from the exam room again.

A few minutes later, another nurse came in and was visibly upset, but was handling it well. She handed me some orders to take with me to the hospital and handed me a piece of paper with my doctor's private number. She also confirmed that the doctor had instructed the staff to give my calls priority. She told me that the entire staff was there for me they were sorry to hear the diagnosis.

EVERYONE who came in that room, were obviously sad and concerned...I've never seen them like this! AND IT SCARED THE *HELL* OUT OF ME EVEN MORE! I mean, HOLEY SOCKS...how *bad* can this *possibly* be?

I gathered my composure as much as I could, splashing cold water on my face in the exam room before I left... and stared at myself in the mirror for a few moments (my left eyelid was almost completely closed). I went to the checkout desk and ask if there's anything else I need to know?

The nurse had told me no and that they were expecting me at the hospital and I was to go there *as soon as possible*. I think I was hugged by everyone there...even another patient who 'overheard' what and *who,* gave me a hug...then, I went home.

By the time I got home it was still setting in... that I have *lung cancer...*"*advanced* lung cancer!" The more I thought about it, the more I was concerned because I had *no medical insurance* and since I had been laid off from work for a while prior, my bank account had been starting to get "a little thin" and I had no idea how am I going to *pay* for *any* of this? I thought to myself, "My God! I'm going to *die* of *cancer* because I can't *afford* the *treatment*?" I didn't know what I was going to do and I didn't know if there was *anything* that *could* be done.

I called my dad and informed him of the diagnosis I had just received although not yet confirmed (*although* I *knew*).

My dad told me to stay *strong* and be *positive* and to let him know if there's anything he could do. Then I called a friend to see if they could take me to the hospital for the MRIs...I had started shaking so bad, I didn't trust my driving. My friend was shocked and of course, agreed to take me to the hospital and asked if they could come over to talk... I said "sure"... but I didn't know what to say or what I *could* say. A short time later my friend drove me to the hospital. Going to the hospital that night was a very "uncomfortable" drive, the closer we got...it really seemed *surreal*...and cold.

I was still shaking as I walked into the radiology/MRI department and presented the orders from my doctor to the nurse. She instructed me to come right in and took me into the MRI room. There, I was instructed to lie down on the MRI table and was positioned quite carefully upon the table.

The MRI technician informed me that the doctor had ordered the MRIs to be "with contrast" and "without contrast". She informed me that the "contrast material" would give me certain feelings and have *certain effects* on my body during the MRI with the contrast being injected into me. I was still scared and wondering just how advanced IS this that it's in/on my lung, that it is damaging my eyes? Is it in my brain too? I asked these questions...the standard response was "I'm so sorry...we can't tell anything yet and the MRIs must be viewed by the doctor, etc." Now, I understand that and respect it...but when you're on the receiving end of a cancer diagnosis, even a *little* information can be worse than *too much*...the *fear* of what you don't know. I had no idea these tests will come out good news or bad news. A cancer diagnosis creates unimaginable uncertainties.

The MRI exams were completed and the MRI tech came in and informed me that the MRI results were to be reviewed immediately and that my doctor was going to be phoned about those results as soon as they were in and that I should expect a phone call from my physician sometime the same evening.

I was home by 8PM...and to this day, I cannot remember anything from the time I left the hospital, to the time my Doctor called.

My friend had contacted two friends who we mutually knew and they were at my home within 15 to 20 minutes of me getting back from the hospital. They're asking me questions as to what symptoms I had and what I was going to do next. They asked how soon I would hear of the MRI results. I simply said "I don't know. The doctor said he would call me as soon as he had the results."

My friends were doing their best to console me and comfort me… but all I could do was just stare down and wonder… and cry… although I *tried* to be strong.

"Be strong". That's what we are *all* told at some point in our life when life gets tough. Where exactly, does "strength" come from? Well, most people will answer that "strength comes from within". An inner strength kind of thing. Is strength learned? Is it either with the person or not? Does it come from one's own faith and beliefs? Is it part of a person's character? I like to think that any "inner strength" is something that I learned from my dad… (just one of *many* things that I learned from him) that I believe is helping me get through this. I also believe that inner strength _is_ part of a person's *character*.

At 9:10 PM that evening the phone rang and it was my doctor. He asked me how I was doing and how I was handling the situation. I told him I didn't know and I hope that he had good news.

He said, "Kev, it's stage IV cancer and *inoperable*". I was in my kitchen taking the call as friends were in my living room, and when he told me this I dropped the phone; I fell to the floor and wept.

Again I regained my composure as best I could and he informed me that he had talked to two separate Oncologists, a thoracic surgeon and the hospital's financial department. He then informed me that the next day I was to go to the hospital to have a PET scan and biopsies done. While in tears, I told him I didn't know how I was going to pay for any of this as he knew I had no insurance. He told me "not to worry about that now" and that I was going to be receiving *excellent* care... and that they were going to get me as much "time" as possible.

*"As much time as possible..." What exactly does that mean?*

My mind was so clouded with the uncertainty ahead and *fear* that I found it difficult just to form simple sentences. Before my doctor hung up, he again assured me that I needed to reach him I could reach him at the private number I was given and someone from his office would be calling me the next morning to give me more information and what I was going to be doing, where I need to go, and what was going to happen... Well, I would find out tomorrow.

Now, I'm thinking of the horror stories that we've all heard about what happens to cancer patients... especially during "late stage" or "end stage"

28

cancer. My thoughts went to my favorite Aunt who had passed away many years earlier of lung cancer. I remember visiting her quite literally on her deathbed, in her home, a day or two before she passed. She looked a fragment of the strong, independent and very loving woman that she was. She looked like an Auschwitz victim. She was bald with just a few strands of errant hair, her skin was a chalky gray and her facial features were quite gaunt as she had lost so much weight. I'm so glad I was able to see her at least one more time before she passed. I whispered to her how sorry I was and that I would do anything to be able to help her. She looked at me very sunken eyes but I can see the love she had her "favorite nephew"... I kissed her forehead and told her how much I loved her and that I would never forget her. I'll always remember the wonderful Christmases we spent at her home when I was a child. It was just truly magical being there for the holidays. When I look back and remember how she looked as cancer ravaged her, I felt that I was seeing my future. And I cried.

After a while, my friends assured me that they would be there for me if I needed anything and then they left.


I don't know how I got to sleep that night.

# Chapter 3

# So It Begins

Early the next morning, I awakened to the sound of my phone ringing and when I answered the phone it was one of the nurses from my doctor's office calling. She informed me that I was to go to the hospital within the next hour to have a PET scan and have biopsies taken. She told me how worried the staff was… and everyone was there for me if I needed anything.

When I arrived at the hospital, I went to the radiology/imaging department and upon signing in, I was immediately taken to a room and asked to remove all clothing and jewelry and put on a hospital gown and someone will be in shortly to take me in to begin the testing. After an approximate 10 minute wait, a nurse came in and briefly described what these tests involve. She informed me that the PET scan will give the doctors a *pinpoint* accurate location of the tumor so a clean biopsy could be taken to determine what "type" of cancer that I was dealing with. She further explained that the biopsy may be "uncomfortable" but wouldn't be too bad and shouldn't take too long. I was placed in a wheelchair and the nurse took me into the imaging area where I was instructed to lay face down on the scan table and was to lie still as I made an initial pass through the machine. After this PET scan was finished, several nurses and what appeared to be two doctors came in with full scrubs and facemasks, wheeling in a tray with very medical looking "instruments" on it. I was then instructed to raise my arms outward above my head where two nurses, one on each arm, grabbed a hold of my wrists and lightly pulled them tight. The doctor then undid my hospital gown from behind and then inserted, with what appeared to be a 'carpenter's nail with a dull tip" into my back between my shoulder blade and spine. This was surprisingly more painful than I had anticipated and it seemed to last for more than 10 or 15 minutes although I'm sure it only took a few minutes, but, as they were doing the procedure they were telling me that they had to place the biopsy needle in a very specific spot to get an adequate sample for analysis.

Seeing *all* these people around me and in the position I was in on this table and *knowing* what they were doing, the *fear* kept building within...I couldn't help but cry more.

On top of all this, I felt like such a "wimp" for crying *so much...* but, being in a situation I found myself *then,* I felt like I *deserved* a good cry. I have never thought it shameful for a man to cry when he hurts, to cry when he's happy. I have always felt that a man is stronger when he is more in touch with his feelings. Today, I was touching every feeling and emotion I had.

After the biopsy, I was returned to the same room where I changed and I was instructed to go ahead and get in bed and relax and that my doctor would be in soon to discuss the biopsy results. My friend who drove me to the hospital for the biopsies was allowed to re-enter the room. They asked me what happened and they asked me how I was feeling. It was so hard to explain what I was feeling with such a flood of emotion going through me. The main emotions I felt were *fear* and *helplessness*.

With what seemed like many hours, was only perhaps one half or one hour. My doctor came into the room and asked my friend they if would step out for a moment. He came up to me with visible tears in his eyes and smile on his face... Which I thought to myself "how can he *possibly* be smiling"? He looked at me and said "Kev, I have some good news! I have reviewed all of the scans and biopsy results and they all show that your cancer "type" is a "*non-small cell cancer*" and that it was a very slow progressing cancer. Furthermore, he informed me that, "non-small cell cancers are easier to treat because of their *slow progression in nature*" and that the scan had showed that the cancer has not *metastasized* "too far..." and that the "stage" is stage IIIA *and* that the two Oncologists and surgeon were waiting to come in and discuss my case with me. My doctor then left the room and upon his leaving the Radiology Oncologist came in and sat down by my bed. The doctor informed me that she had seen all of my tests, all of my scans and the biopsy results and confirmed what my doctor had said that the cancer had *not* spread too far. She informed me that the following day I was to come back to the hospital and have a "body mold' made (for

33

positioning me for radiation) and a "Mediport" surgically implanted in my chest for chemotherapy infusion. Also, that my treatment would begin the following Monday in the morning. She asked if I had any questions and at that time I said no. The doctor told me not to worry as she left.

The next Oncologist who came into my room, which seemed like I was having a parade of doctors, came in and sat down next to my bed, introduced himself as a Hematology Oncologist and that he also had reviewed all my records, scans and biopsies and also confirmed the stage and nature of my tumor. He advised me the same thing the Radiologist Oncologist told me that treatment would be *combined* radiation treatment and chemotherapy and would run *concurrently* for five days a week for the next 3 months. After that, they would consult with the surgeon to see if the cancer has been reduced enough in size by radiation and chemo for a successful surgery to remove the damaged portion of my lung and any surrounding tissue damage and at that time, evaluate to see if all treatments to that point leading to surgery were successful. What I've been feeling and experiencing the last day was not subsiding, but it *was* comforting to see that my doctor had contacted perhaps the best in their fields, and in this area, to help me beat the cancer.

Again, when asked if I had any questions, I said no and the second Oncologist left wishing me well and reassuring me that they are doing everything they can to help me.

Now it was time for the surgeon to come in and give me *his* opinion on my condition and tell me what he was going to do.

The surgeon came and sat down on the bed next to mine, introduced himself, and proceeded to repeat the same information that I had received from the other three doctors regarding my situation. He said the PET scans and other test results look promising, *however*, he warned that the tumor was *very* large and it was in a *very* bad place! He informed me that the tumor was laying on the outside surface of my lung (a "Pancoast" tumor) and was growing *laterally* towards the "nerve ganglion" running up my spinal column and explained that this is what has caused my eyelid droop, chronic pain between my shoulder blades in my spine, and the intermittent spasms my left thumb I was having. He further explained the tumor was *starting* to metastasize (spread) to my spine and the nerves surrounding it in that region. He also, quite cautiously, noted the fact it was *precariously* close to my *heart* as well. This is something I *didn't* need to hear. He made a comment that the tumor was *"very large"* and that if the radiation does *not* shrink the tumor enough that surgery would be *impossible*. He then asked me, as did the other doctors, if I had any questions. This time I had a few questions and was actually afraid to ask. Whereas I feel I probably should have asked the first two Oncologists, I asked the surgeon *exactly* what does radiation and chemo *do*? He told me that chemotherapy is used to kill any cancer cells that may have been "shed" (when cancer cells 'break-away') from the tumor and circulated throughout my body through my bloodstream. He told me that the radiation is intended to kill the *tumor* and shrink it to a manageable and surgically removable size. He then informed me that the Mediport was to be used because I was going to receive a large amount of chemotherapy for many weeks and that it would be easier on me, to have the Mediport so that I wouldn't have to be continually jabbed by what he described as "a large bore IV needle" each time I have a chemo *infusion*. My next question to him was "Doctor, am I going to survive this?" His response was, "I wouldn't go out and buy a funeral plot if I were you." He then smiled, shook my hand, and as he left he patted me on the leg and said "hang in there and I will see you soon".

After the surgeon had left, my friend who drove me to the hospital came back into the room sat down next to me.

They told me they were talking with my doctor in the hallway and that my doctor actually had tears in his eyes when he told them how glad he was that he was able to give me *better news* than he had given me the night before. My doctor came back into the room and sat down beside me and, the same as the other doctors, asked if I any questions and if there's anything he could do. I told him no, and I think I thanked him over and over for being there for me and that I appreciated *everything* that he has done and is doing on my behalf. I again told my doctor how afraid I was for my life for the fact that I could not afford medical treatment and was worried as to how much everything has cost so far. He smiled and placed his hand on my shoulder and said "don't worry about that now Kev." He said this hospital is a "religious affiliated" hospital and will *not deny* you excellent medical care because you are unable to pay and that my treatments would begin *immediately*.

With that, he smiled and shook my hand and told me to call his office or to call his private line and there's *anything* I needed.

I talked with my friend for a moment, while waiting for someone to come in and tell me I can go home, about what the previous doctors had discussed with me. My friends eyes teared up as I described the procedures I was about to begin the following Monday. A nurse, I presume, came in and handed me several sheets of instructions and information that I was going to need for the surgery I was going to have. Since I had no questions for her, I was informed that I could go home and advised to read *all* the material I was just given in preparation for the surgery. She did her best to reassure me that the doctors that had just seen were the *best* and that they would do *everything* and *anything* they could to take care of me and help me through this. I thanked her, she gave me a hug and a smile, I got dressed and as I was leaving I thanked the nurses and the staff that had been so nice and helpful while I was there. My friend drove me home... in what seemed to be such a long drive home... and a *silent* one. Neither of us knew what to say.

When I got home I called my dad, explained that the test procedure was about, explained what the doctors had told me and let him know of the surgery I was going to get the following Monday. As was his style, in his calm voice, he told me to relax, get some sleep and don't worry. He said if there is anything that I needed to just call them... he told me he loved me... I asked him to explain to mom as gentle as possible so she wouldn't worry and then we hung up.

I called my best friend who lives in Arizona and give him the news. I could tell by his voice that he was very upset. As we were talking I heard him tell his wife that I had cancer and how severe it was, in the background I could hear her say "Oh my God! No!" I felt so bad having to tell him that and now having his *family* know this; it broke my heart because my friend and his family are very close to me. I gave him as much information as I knew and he told me to take care and that his wife says that they love me and are praying for me. I gave him and his family my love and told them and keep in touch and I would let them know what was going on. My friend said "You *better*, Mister!" I told him I wasn't going to say goodbye, rather, talk to you soon.

Once everybody had left, and I made calls to those I thought should know, I began thinking "what if I don't make it through this?" Who would take care of my cats, Sweetie and Puddin? You see, my cats are *very important part of my life*. Since I was never fortunate enough to have children of my own and having a lot of love inside of me to give, and gave that love to them. Anyone who knows me knows that I don't do anything unless I can give it 100%. If it's my artwork, 100%. When it comes to my family, friends and loved ones, 100%. When it comes to my cats, 100%.

And if I am fortunate enough, one day meet that *special woman*, I would give my best and 100%. *Always!* ☺This has been my mindset for many years since I *must* stay true to myself and my beliefs, I will *not* compromise these beliefs and I *will* apply them for the upcoming events... *100%.*

And what should I do about my house, car and belongings? What do I do with my *golf clubs*? I thought to myself, that I should make a will. The only good thing that I could think of is the fact that my funeral arrangements have been made in advance.

As much as I like to focus on the *positive* in life, after the diagnosis of lung cancer, I just *couldn't* see *any* positive *anywhere*. From the time my Doctor told me that he suspected a *serious form of lung cancer*, with *complications*, some *positive* did make itself clear. Since I'm rather particular to *who* I consider as a "friend", the friends who *were* there for me gave me my first glimpse of hope through their encouragement, their kindness and their offers *of* help if I needed. Words can't describe the pain in my heart for causing my friend's who I love and care for, so much worry. It hurts me *more* to know that my illness is hurting people I care about.

I also have some close neighbors here who are Seniors and I try to look out for them, check up on and help them if I can. I mean, I have no idea how long any of these treatments are going the last, what was going to happen to me during these treatments and *if* I'm still going to be able to help the seniors by shoveling the snow, or taking them leftovers, or just stopping by to see how they are... well, if I am unable to do this I will feel like I'm letting them down. And what if I'm unable to go to my parents? I always used to go to their home at least two or three times a week to make them a nice dinner (prior to my diagnosis), fix things around the house anything that needed fixing, visit with them and my brother of course... I feel as though I will let them down as well. Of course, I know they will understand and do anything they can to help, my parents are seniors and my brother has enough to worry about on his own without any of them having to be worried about me. I know it's a *family thing*, but I still feel bad for bringing *my* troubles into *their* life. It truly scares me to feel that there's a *very good chance* the time may come that I may not be there for my friends and family and loved ones when they need me.

As for my little furry companions, Sweetie and Puddin, I *know* that my trusted and long time friend who is a veterinarian and has taken such awesome care of my little ones in the past, that he would find them kind and loving homes in case I'm unable to care for them any longer. Makes me very sad to know that it's a possibility that my lil furbabies won't be able to play or take naps with Papa (me), get their nighttime treats the way we always do, and they always enjoy.

These last two days have been the worst possible days of my life. By me *knowing* of what happens to people with cancer, the *treatments* and *torture* they go through, and now *knowing* the emotional turmoil...and...facing the real possibility of my death has me completely drained inside.

41

My heart feels heavy, my soul feels empty and this damn pain in my back keeps getting worse.

# Chapter 4

# The First Wave

    Today is the first Monday after my diagnosis. I can't remember very much of anything from the past weekend except sadness and *fear*. The weekend is lost to me (to this day); fear has an amazing ability to "blot out time", to make time "non-existent". I *know* that a few friends and my family called or visited me every day prior to the upcoming Monday...I simply cannot remember *anything*...except *fear*.

I hope that doesn't make me sound selfish or looking for "pity"...it just seems that my *mind* was simply so clouded with the damn *fear*, that I could only focus on the "what now's" and "what if's"...that follow *fear*. In my *mind*...I seemed to be somehow *preparing* for the *reality* of my *death*. Forgive me for saying; this is a *hell* of a thing to have to accept as a very *real* possibility! Of course, I tried *desperately* to find *any* possibility to *prevent* dying...the damn *fear* was just so strong and so soon after diagnosis. I *knew* that I had family; friends and *excellent* Dr's...the biopsies, scans and the *knowledge* of what I was going to have to do to live were quite terrifying. (when you hear the word "cancer" and "your name" in the same sentence...your mind *immediately* brings the memories of people you've known who have gone through (or died) from cancer...and the "treatments" and the "effect's"...I mean, I understood this first surgery is "routine"... *but it was just getting started...*

Today is the day I have surgery to place a Mediport in my chest. This device is to be *surgically joined* with the main artery in my chest to allow delivery of chemotherapy to my bloodstream through a "port" which has a small tube that extends through my skin, having a receptacle on the end of this to which the chemotherapy needle is to be inserted. This is intended, (due to the many upcoming infusions) by saving me from having to endure many, daily "needle sticks" that will be required for me to receive chemo infusions.

I arrived at the hospital at 5:30 AM and reported to the surgical department. I signed in and was taken to a room where I was to prepare for the surgery by undressing the putting on the *humorous* and albeit *too revealing hospital gown*. It was cold this morning so I decided to go ahead and utilize the bed. Within a few moments the nurse came in and proceeded take my vitals. She informed me that a pre-op physician will be coming in to talk with me and discuss the procedure with me.

An elderly physician walked in and introduced himself with a very heavy German accent and he greets me in English and asked me what I know about the procedure I am about to receive. Barely being able to remember the German classes I took in junior high school, I was able to wish him a good morning and asked how he was doing in German. A big smile came to his face and without hesitation began talking to me in German, whereas I had to interrupt him with the *limited* German I knew in response and told him "I'm sorry but my German is not very good". He laughed and told me the German that I was able to speak was pronounced properly and he said that I had a "Bavarian accent!" I was actually amazed that I understood some of what he was saying but not all of it. Better yet, he actually understood *my* German! ☺

After our limited conversation "auf Deutsche" (in German) he informed me that the surgeon and the surgical team are ready for me and that a nurse would be coming by shortly to take me back. He could tell that I was scared and worried, and it seems like, with the assurance you get from your grandfather, he patted my leg and told me I would be fine. He said goodbye and hope to see you again *in German*. He smiled; he winked and left the room. At the same time the doctor was leaving the room a nurse came in pushing a wheelchair. At this point, I was asked to sit in the wheelchair and assured that my personal belongings will be looked after and was wheeled into the pre-op ward. I then was put on an operating room table and an IV was placed in my arm.

The surgical nurse told me it was just something to help me relax prior to surgery. Within a few minutes my surgeon arrived, walking up to me in full surgical garb, and gave me details of *exactly* what he was about to do. He told me it was a very safe procedure and that he had done many of them without complications. That was reassuring... *to a point*. (at the initial surgical consultation, the surgeon said I had a '10-15% chance of not making it through surgery'!) I'll take those odds. The surgeon shook my hand and left to prepare for the surgery. There, the anesthesiologist explained the procedure for putting me under in preparation for my surgery. He injected something into the access port on the IV drip that I had and asked me to count backwards from 100. I remember reaching 95... And that was it. (I wonder...do they dress like this for surgery so they can't be identified later at the trial?) ☺

I don't know what time it was when I woke up in the recovery room, but I was told the surgery took 2 hours. I was told the surgery was a success without complication. I was then instructed in how to care for and protect the portion of the Mediport that was hanging outside of my chest. There was a special kind of covering that I was to use to keep the port clean and dry between infusions (this damn thing looks so weird sticking out of my chest!)

After a couple hours a nurse came in and handed me instruction sheets and explained that the area that just had surgery may be tender and/or painful for a day or so. I was also informed that I would begin chemotherapy *and* radiation treatments starting *tomorrow* at 10 AM at the cancer center and was told I should get their an hour early because I was to have a "body mold" made to accommodate positioning me during the radiation. I then was allowed to go home and was told the rest, take it easy and be careful of lying on, bumping or disturbing the port. Later that evening my friend came by to see how is doing and asked about the surgery. I showed them the Mediport and the protective covering I was given. It really looked nasty. But I knew this simple device that was just implanted in my body was going to save me from unnecessary needles. I commented that "it's a good thing that I was never a 'junkie' and shot drugs into my veins, because of the way I *despise* needles." That night, I was very paranoid about bumping or disturbing the surgical implant...needless to say it was a restless night.

The following morning I go to the cancer center, sign in and then go to the radiation department. Upon entering the radiation department my vitals will be taken, I will be given a specific "card" that I was to use to identify myself upon arrival each morning to the radiation department. What it did, was electronically notify staff that I had arrived, note the time, and allowed staff adequate time to get my files and get things ready.

*The next day the treatments are to begin.*

# Chapter 5

# The Second Wave

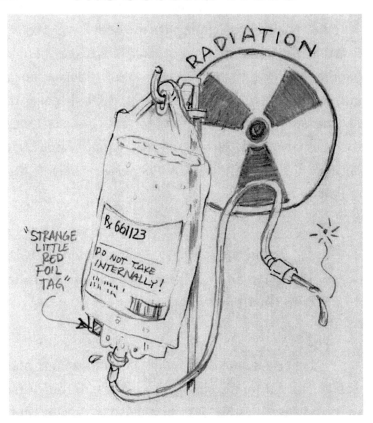

Waking up this morning, I started thinking about what was going to happen today. I'm supposed to go to the cancer center a half hour early and register before I go into radiation. From what I understand this is so the labs and the nursing stations can prepare the chemotherapy drugs and get things ready for my infusion that day.

While I was sitting at the registration desk, I started shaking as I tried to fill out forms that I was given. I actually began to have tears from the sheer fear of what was going to happen. How was this "chemo" going to feel going into my body? What will it do? Will it kill me outright (as I have heard about other patients who didn't survive chemo!) The receptionist attempted to assure me that it everything is going to be fine and if I need anybody to talk to while I was there, that could be arranged. I appreciated but declined the offer and took my paperwork over to the radiation department.

*The following is a detailed account of both chemo and radiation treatments that I would be doing for the next 3 months.*

I checked into the radiology department and was led to the men's changing area was through my shirt and jewelry and put on a hospital gown, then wait for my name to be called. Once my name was called, a nurse would ask my name and date of birth, just for verification purposes I'm sure and then proceeded to lead me in to the room where the radiation treatment would take place. It was behind a very large, 2 foot thick metal door, which was the entrance to the treatment room. A nurse or radiation technician walked over to a locker and opened it and pulled out the foam mold that was made the day before and placed it on the bed portion of the radiation device.

She then instructed me to get up on the table and lie flat and get comfortable, and raise my left arm so settles and comfortably along with my head shoulders and upper body in the mold. She asked if I was okay and I replied "yes". She then left the room and closed the large metal door behind her. That door made a nasty sounding "thunk" as it closed.

Then the treatment began. A lot of mechanical and electrical noises followed, as the device positioned itself over my tumor and began administering the radiation. At first I couldn't feel anything during these treatments. But as time went on... I started to feel it. It wasn't good. The treatment lasted roughly 15-20 minutes. I could never tell how long each session lasted...

After the treatment was over, the large door was opened, and to nurses came in, help me off the table and into wheelchair. Then, back out to the waiting area where I was then able to go to the men's changing room and get dressed. It's a weird feeling *knowing* that the people around you have cancer in *their* bodies and that you *yourself* have cancer in *your* body as well. You can see it in the face of every person sitting in the waiting area that is wearing a hospital gown… *Fear*! And that *not one* patient in there could escape it.

I got dressed and left the radiation department… only to have to go upstairs and have *poison* pumped into my body in the infusion center.

I wondered "what would this stuff feel like? Will it "burn"? Considering what I have read and heard…it *wasn't* looking good…

Upon entering the infusion center I was greeted by a friendly nurse with a clipboard that had my file. She led me to a chair that appeared to be comfortable and asked that I sit down and she would be back within a moment. When I walked into the main room, there were so many other patients receiving chemotherapy, some had family members there, some were alone like myself. I sat down in a chair that looked comfortable but turned out not to be. When she returned she had a little basket filled all sorts of bandages, tapes, tubes and syringes. She was also carrying two. Large IV bags, each having this mysteriously *weird red foil sticker* on it (the chemo used was called 'Cisplatin'…at least that's how it's pronounced). I'm surprised it didn't have a little *skull and cross bones* as well. She proceeded to hang the IV bags on an IV stand and then threaded the tubing through some sort of monitoring device, which I'm presuming monitors and regulates the flow of chemo into my port.

She then pulled out what appeared to be a very large needle and connected it to the tubes she then inserted the needle in the port in my chest. She taped down the tubing so wouldn't move the needle out of the port by accident. She then informed me that the chemo was being administered and the process would take up to 6½ hours to complete. She then also reminded me that this will be the same procedure every day until this course of chemo was completed.

She informed me that the first infusion would last 6½ hours (On Mondays) and 4 ½ hours on the other days (Tuesday thru Friday). All the while that the chemo was being fed into my body I kept thinking of the words of the Oncologist of the possible oncoming effects. When do they start? How bad would they be? And what was I going to be able to do about the side effects? What seemed to be an eternity, of listening to daytime TV shows, and conversations throughout the room, today passed very, very slowly. I kept looking at the bags, hanging on the IV stand and watch them eventually drain into me over the course of 6 ½ hours.

All the while…I feel *alone*, in a room *full* of people, I feel *so alone*. I saw families and loved one there with other patients…and I felt *really weird* sitting there alone...except the occasional nurse checking on me.

During the infusions, sometimes I would wander about...(dragging this contraption pumping poison in me along...even to the *bathroom*!)...I would check out this little space that had Catholic rosaries, pamphlets of support, things of that nature, and I stopped and looked at the rosaries...and started thinking about God.

Whereas I never considered myself as "religious", rather, more of a "spiritualist"..."Agnostic" is the term for it...anyway, I would never "pray" for myself...but I would pray for others on occasion. By seeing the love and support the other patients were getting, I saw a few prayers answered right then!

There were a few times where I seriously thought "God may be a little too busy for me..."and left it at that. That may seem a harsh or "negative" statement...but it was true as to the way I saw it at the time. It's not a 'good thing, bad thing' thought, simply the way it is!

The whole time, during this, the first of many "infusions", I would look around at the other patients. Not knowing their diagnosis or stage of cancer, and I would look at their *eyes*. As much as I could *see* the *courage* in those eyes...I saw the *exact fear* I felt inside. It was a very scary and humbling experience.

Even though the first couple weeks I tried very hard to not make direct eye contact…it was very clear to see.

It was almost 5 o'clock by the time the bags had emptied and a nurse unplugged me from the IV bags and told me to have a good day and that she would see me again tomorrow. It's funny as it may sound, even after the very first chemo infusion; I actually believe I could feel this stuff coursing through my body. It was a very *uncomfortable* feeling.

There were a wide variety of people that were receiving chemo treatments.

Young, old, men, women; there is no discrimination when it comes to cancer. *Anyone* can get it!

The first few days of chemo, I didn't speak to anyone because I didn't know what to say. I didn't know how they would react to me. When I noticed anybody looking at me, I would simply give a slight nod and then try to take a nap if possible. Also, as the treatments continued I was always feeling quite cold and would on occasion ask for a blanket. There are usually several other patients who had blankets as well.

At the end of the infusion session, the nurse came back removed all the IV tubing and covered my port with a sterile cover. She advised me to keep the port dry when showering and she told me I needed to drink plenty of fluids between treatment sessions.

As I drove home I kept wondering "how can I do this every day?" (After just a couple weeks in I thought that the treatment I was undergoing wasn't going to work. How can anything that makes you feel like *this,* possibly do any good?)

When I returned home, had attempted to eat, my appetite wasn't really there due to the stress and *fear* of everything, I still had to eat. Apparently, the stories I have heard about what chemotherapy does to you became all too true. Within an hour of eating dinner, I had the urge to vomit, which was overwhelming and I was barely able to make it in the bathroom in time. Are you *kidding* me?

*ON THE VERY FIRST DAY?*

This was going to happen, from now on until the chemotherapy is completed and going to be a daily ritual. As soon as the urge to have to run to the bathroom to throw up subsided, and my stomach was obviously emptied at this point, I decided to relax, watching TV and attempt to sleep.

The day, so far, wasn't as bad as I thought it would be as the days went on however, the nausea, the sickness, constant shaking/shivering, the weight loss and hair loss seems to happen at an increasing rate. HAIR LOSS?

The next morning when I woke up and was preparing to go to the cancer center on what was to be a long and difficult time, while dressing I had noticed they were small tufts of my hair on my pillow! I couldn't believe it was happening so soon. I called my friend who has been my hair stylist for the last several years and informed her of what was going on. I could tell she was upset on the phone as I asked to make an appointment so I could come in and have her remove all my hair. Again, I just couldn't stand the idea of walking around with patches of hair, patches of bald spots on my head. Of course, I knew I could always wear a baseball hat and that it would hide most of the balding. But I still didn't want to chance it and I went to have my hair cut after the chemo and radiation session for that day.

After that day's treatment, my friend was able to take me in rather quickly, as I walked in I could see her eyes welling up with tears and she said she could see the *fear* in my eyes. I was totally embarrassed by wearing a surgical face mask to keep myself from germs. My friend then started to tell me about the loss of her brother the previous year from brain cancer. She said it brought back all the memories of that when she saw me walk in the face mask on. I sat down in the chair, and she questioned my decision to have my hair cut off. I told her she should "shave it to the bone" and answered as many of the questions as to what was going on as I could. Some questions brought tears, others did not.

My friend cried the whole time she was shaving my head. When she was done she asked me if I want to see if I said no. I then attempted to pay her for the haircut and she came and gave me a big hug and told me she couldn't accept any money for this. She then, knowing how I am, told me she was not going to take no for an answer! With that I gave her another hug, thanked her so much for listening and cutting my hair. She told me she's going to pray for me and asked me to keep in touch if I could let her how I was. As I left I noticed a tear streamed down her face as she tried to put on a smile, I did the same. While driving home, I kept removing my hat and running my hand over my head. This is the *first* time in my life, since I was just a baby, that I had absolutely *no hair* on my head. It felt too weird for words.

By the second week, the effects of chemotherapy were making themselves *very* well known. During infusions my bones felt like they had acid coursing through each bone. Every muscle in my body was in *pain*...they felt like they were being *shredded* and *pulled from my bones*. My skin felt like I was made of old papier-mâché. Anything I tried to eat, but wasn't able to keep down, tasted like fouled cardboard. My sense of smell was completely gone. Every joint in my body felt as though there was broken glass between the joints. This is <u>no</u> exaggeration! This is as accurate of a description as I can give.

I thought to myself "...and I have got three more months of this?"

And it didn't stop after the tube was pulled out...it just to seem more intense during that actual infusion.

*This was not going to be easy...but I must stay focused and positive...and "BE STRONG"!*

It's time for me to *more* become focused and concentrate on the *positive* around me. Whether it is from my family and friends, other people, doctors and nurses, or other patients... or maybe just a kind act from a stranger, an understanding smile or maybe from just one sincere hug. With whatever happens, I have to remain true to *myself* and true to my "life philosophy", and be *strong*. (Yup...there's that word *again*!) It's just another "do the *right* thing, for the *right* reason". You must be true to *yourself* and *be content* with the *person* who you *are*, as opposed to being the person *others* would have you be. We cannot, and *do not* have the right to judge, control, or tell others how to live their lives. By living life and being the best you that *you* can be and stay in control and true to *your* own life, that is your life's example and ultimately your legacy. We can only control *our own lives* in the direction that we take.

*Thinking this way will prove and has proven to serve me quite well.*

Since chemo is administered into your blood (thru the Mediport) and is distributed to *every cell in your body*, it not only has an effect on you *physically* but *neurologically* as well. And the whole ordeal with the diagnosis of *advanced lung cancer* and everything about to happen, the *emotional damage* was just starting as well. Over the course of my radiation/chemo treatments I began to notice changes not only through my body by losing over 40 pounds in the first month, losing my hair, my sense of taste and sense of smell, I noticed that my hearing acuity had increased quite a bit. I also discovered that I had a persistent "ringing in my ears" and noticed that I remembered more dreams and that those dreams were *extremely vivid* and *detailed*.

I didn't know it at the time, but I have been told that I would have "lapses in memory" and "behave" differently than I normally would have. I learned this was called "chemo fog" and that the majority of chemo patients are affected by this as well, especially for those going through "aggressive treatments" like I was. When I discussed these symptoms or "side-effects" with my Oncologist seemed *very* surprised when I told her of the *increase* in my hearing capabilities. She informed me that normally, *most* patients actually *lose* a portion if not *most* of their hearing while going through chemo treatments and that these could be either temporary or permanent, or, either improve or get worse over time. Because chemo affects each person differently, the subsequent side effects and physical or neurological damage caused is unpredictable at best. Okay then... with my rather *unique* circumstances, I seem to be one for the books!

I always *did* like doing things *differently* than most...the way things *should* be done. The *right* way and for the *right* reasons!

My Oncologist then recommended that I take *very specific* vitamins, minerals and supplements to boost my immune system during the radiation/chemo treatments. And I continue with these supplements and vitamins to this day. (More specific details will be given later in this book).

So this is how it went for 3 months. My total weight loss was...from about 175 pounds (and in pretty good shape) to 130 pounds in a month or so! Although protein shakes got me back to a better weight prior to surgery...I had muscle loss as well. It's called "cachexia" (wasting syndrome). This is such a danger to anyone going through chemo/radiation. Understanding this, I had to make daily trips to the store for "Ensure"...I *lived* on these things...the *chocolate*...and I believe they helped.

As I had *just* started golfing and had asked my oncologist and family Doctor if I could golf...at least *try* to golf? They both enthusiastically said "sure, just be careful and take it easy"! Really? ☺

This is where my golf buddy suggested a smaller, 9-hole course to get out, get some exercise...practice! It's good therapy, yeah? It was better than lying in bed all day!

I had gotten myself to this lil 9-hole and used a power cart. (now, it was a small course, but the chemo and radiation had left me very weak, and nauseous...but I just HAD to get out of the house! I was able to drive there, but then trying to concentrate on my golf swing like feeling pain and sick...was a challenge!

And I was *able to do it!* NOT very well...and I lost a few balls...but I completed the *whole 9!* No... I won't tell you what I shot on a par 31-9 hole! ☺

All through my initial chemo/radiation, I was able to go for a couple hours at a time on weekends when I didn't have treatments. After a few times, a few of the "older regulars" there asked me to join them. I explained I was not very good and...uh..."sick". (I was still wearing the mask during all this to avoid germs-immune system gone from chemo-so it was obvious I was sick!) but they welcomed me anyway.

One fellow realized it was cancer...his wife was a survivor *twice* over...so he had a "soft spot" for me I guess. He would offer encouragement on my shots, a tip here or there. However...there was *one* of those "regulars" who just *didn't* like me playing with them (I *presumed* it was I was *lousy* at golf) but later found out, he didn't realize I was fighting cancer! Well...I must say, the following golf season, I ran into those older regulars...and to my complete shock, the gentleman who was rather nasty the previous year, was the first to say "hello" shake my hand AND tell me he was *glad to see me*! REALLY? ☺ As it turns out, during the off-season, a couple of the other fellows really told this guy off! They "guilted" the heck out of him...saying "how could you be so mean to a guy fighting cancer and WANTS to try and golf...and maybe learn from *you*?" (that was an exact quote from the manager of the course!) This "now chastised" fellow had simply said he didn't *know*! He *thought* I was just a crappy golfer! (HA! Thought so!) ☺

Although there were a few times...when people didn't understand...or who didn't care...where I found it difficult to handle it! BUT...I also experienced man, many kindnesses that helped me along the way...

There were several occasions where shopping trips were scary. Since I would go shopping on the way home from treatments...some days I *should* have went straight home. It kind of bothered me seeing children staring at the 'scary man in the mask' ... my skin was chalky, dark around my eyes, clothes not fitting through the weight loss... (Yeah, I looked scary to *them* and to *myself*.) I looked like an emaciated Uncle Fester. I tried to avoid letting kid's see me...but there was one time where I didn't have a choice. One particular day, I was feeling worse than usual...I actually had to *sit on the floor* in the store before I fell. It was VERY embarrassing. I couldn't even hold myself up on the cart! Sure, several people came over concerned of course, I just felt so...*helpless*!

There were many situations and incidents that occurred but the point here is that somehow, I was finding that *'strength thing'* people are telling me to find!

All during this "first round"...there were *terrifying* moments on a *daily* basis. Extreme sense of being very cold, sweating sometime so much that I had to change sheets often and lay bath towels under me, *excruciating* pain throughout my entire body, EXTREMELY VIVID dreams...and *nightmares*; so *real* to *me* it was as if in a blink of my eyes, I was between *reality* and *dream/nightmare*. I was afraid to sleep because I didn't know if I was going to dream or have nightmares! There were moments where I had to *crawl* to the bathroom or kitchen because I was so weak.

Each day turned into night and time seemed to have no meaning. The only "time" I noticed was what time I had to go to the cancer center...a time I learned to *fear*.

There were three specific days that had noteworthy events.

The first, was one day while changing for radiation, I noticed a very thin, very frightened looking man who appeared to be in his early 40s with a feeding tube port protruding from his stomach. I asked if he minded if I asked what type of cancer he had. He told me he had "esophageal cancer" and said it was caused by "excess consumption of alcohol." Well, for some reason I felt the need to talk to him further. We introduced ourselves to each other and I found his name was Howard. He seemed like a very likable fellow but I couldn't help but notice the *fear* in his eyes. It seemed more intense than most of the other patients. So on the second day that I had seen Howard, I brought him a copy of my first book[1] in the hopes that it could take away some of his fear and help him deal with his treatments and start feeling a little better about himself. It seemed to work too. As the days passed, Howard seemed as though he was handling things much better. His caregiver even mentioned to me that he was indeed feeling better and was having a better outlook on his life.

I believe I only saw Howard in the radiation department for couple weeks and then I didn't see him anymore. I couldn't find anybody that could tell me how he was doing. I hope he is doing well... I hope he became a cancer survivor. ☺

There was another occasion while at the radiation department, whereas when I came out of the changing room to have a seat, I saw another one of my elderly neighbors in a hospital gown!

As soon as I noticed him (he couldn't see me because he was mostly blind) his wife *had* noticed *me*! She's a sweet little lady that stands about "5 feet nuthin"...and she ran up to me and threw her arms around me and asked me what I was doing there? Well, since I hadn't mentioned my cancer to *any* of my neighbors because I did NOT want them to worry... looks like the cat is out of the bag! She then walked me over to her husband and announced the fact that I was there and he put his hand out to shake my hand and of course I shook his hand, then he asked me what I was doing there. His wife filled him in and he told me how sorry he was. I did my best to assure them both and I was doing fine and that they should concentrate on *his* treatment and not to worry about me. Since I was not feeling my best anyway that day, I needed to leave as soon as I could, so I told them if there was anything I can do to help, that they knew where I lived and could call me anytime.

My neighbor only had 10 days of radiation. He did not have any chemo and I never knew what type of cancer he had. But he is in his mid 80s, so it couldn't be good.

I wished them both a good day and offered some reassurance to them, and they both gave me a big hug as I was leaving and told me to take care.

Now since I live in a nice little neighborhood where everybody tries to keep their lawn just one notch above the neighbors, and everybody knew each other, I *knew* my neighbors would tell *other* neighbors and the news of me being at the cancer center would reach all of the *other* neighbors in *less* than an hour. We have a very nice, quiet, safe and *friendly* street. For instance, in the winter after there has been a pileup of snow, I would crank up my trusty snow blower and first I would do the seniors right across the street first. Remember, *this* neighbor is *very* particular about keeping his driveway clean and free of snow or ice. So I always do his driveway and sidewalk *first* (mainly because he used to try and shovel himself...and since I couldn't bare the sight of him frozen in his driveway...I would do it before he could get to it! I had to ask his dear wife to sit on him...and keep him inside!) so after I'm done doing mine, if he wants an adjustment I can take care of it! After their shoveling was complete I would proceed to do a senior two houses down. And since I had to make a path *anyways* to get to her sidewalk from line, well, I figured as long as I am out here maybe my other neighbors would like a clear sidewalk in the morning.

I would finish that, then come home and do my own driveway and sidewalk. Now of course I didn't do their *entire* driveways but I did make sure that sidewalk leading up to the porch was clean and the approach to the driveway by the street was clear so they could get in and out of the driveways.

Mind you, I'm *not* complaining or *bragging*, the exercise *alone* was worth it and the good feeling about helping your neighbors and friends is just in the spirit of our neighborhood. Okay, I admit, I do it simply because it makes *me* feel good *to* do it for my neighbors. And ... I *know* they would do it for me. In fact a good neighbor several houses down shoveled my sidewalk and driveway so wouldn't have to (when I was in treatment) and I hired someone to take care of my lawn in the spring because I *knew* I would be too weak and tired to do it. Anyone who knows me *knows* how *ridiculous* I am about keeping my lawn looking nice.

Then there was one of the biggest scares of this whole ordeal that happened while having radiation therapy at about five weeks into treatments.

After completing what seemed like just another radiation treatment, I felt there was trouble because when the nurses came in to help me off the radiation table I *couldn't move!* I couldn't raise my head or use my arms or legs to try and push myself up off of the table. My eyes were twitching rapidly side to side, uncontrollably and I felt "pins and needles" were poking me all over my body. I explained this to the nurses and they asked me to try again to get off of the table and were checking my eyes at the same time. After helping me into the wheelchair, literally having to pick me up and set me in the chair, one nurse left the room in a hurry and the other nurse began wheeling me out of the treatment room. I'm not sure of a timeframe, but when I got out to the waiting area there were two EMT people there with a gurney waiting for me. My neighbors (who I mentioned before) where there as well as the EMT's carefully loaded me onto the gurney and strapped me in and rushed me down to the entrance where the ambulance was waiting. They informed me that they are going to take me to the emergency room at the hospital... which was just across the parking lot from the cancer center. I thought to myself, "good grief! All this fuss just to go a few hundred yards?" I was taken, by *ambulance* no less to the hospital's ER! *This cracked me up!*

The EMT guys advised the doctors and nurses that I had come from cancer center and I remember hearing the nurses telling them that the cancer center had called ahead. They didn't even take me off of the ambulance gurney and wheeled me straight in to the MRI room. The MRI was performed and they were focused on just scanning my *head.* As I was rather upset and concerned at this, my heart seemed to grow cold as I thought "I have *cancer* in my *brain* now."

*I honestly felt that my time had run out.*

*I felt very cold and very alone...again.*

After the MRI the nurse got me into wheelchair and proceeded to wheel me into a private exam room within the ER. She then came back and had several "juice boxes" and told me to drink as many as possible, as soon as possible (they said I was *extremely* dehydrated). She then informed me that the Doctor will be with me in a couple minutes to advise me of what's going on. Despite all that was going on at this time, when the Doctor *did* come in, I was totally shocked! As it turns out she was an *incredibly* cute blonde! I thought to myself "okay, things are getting a *little* bit better!" ☺ She introduced herself and explained that they (The doctor at the cancer center) were concerned that I may have cancer or *something else* in my brain that was causing the symptoms I had immediately following that last radiation treatment.

She said the radiology department was a little busy that day but that they would have results as soon as they could, she had ordered them STAT and she would come and tell me what those results were.

As I was sitting in that little ER room when another doctor had come in and asked me why I was there explained to him my diagnosis and how far along I was in treatment. He gave me words of encouragement and then informed me that the hospital I was at was a "teaching hospital" and asked if I would mind if he brought some medical students in to give me a quick evaluation. He asked that I did not tell them anything and that I was just to sit there and let them examine me. I agreed and told him no problem. Shook my hand and thanked me and left the room. Within about 10 minutes the doctor returned with a whole gaggle of about seven medical students. All carrying clipboards and in the traditional white coats they begin looking at me, taking my statistics, blood pressure, heart rate, temperature, lungs and then a visual examination. They also examined my reflexes and flexibilities and I heard one of the students mention hearing a slight "crunching" sound while manipulating my left arm. The doctor then announced "times up" and ushered them out of the room, thanking me along the way and several students also expressed thanks. I gave a slight wave and a smile and "you're welcome". After even more waiting in the small room, with no food all that day, closing in to around 7:00 PM, I was actually getting hungry! So, no food, but the one Doctor did come back. He told me that only a few of the students caught the arthritis in my left shoulder and that the rest of them observed no abnormalities whatsoever and reported "nothing unusual presented"... then he told me they were all going to get chewed out, because they didn't notice the Horner's syndrome (eye lid droop) or the hair loss, not to mention the burn mark on the upper left side of my chest (from radiation). We laughed about the Doctor going to chew out the med students and I had asked him to go easy on them. He agreed. Before he left he had told me he had looked at my chart and offered me assurance that I would be okay. He gave me a pat on the arm, shook my hand, thanked me again and left the room.

So as I'm waiting for results, every once in a while a different nurse would pop in to see if I was doing okay. I had asked one nurse if there's any way I could get something to eat. She replied since it's late she didn't know where she could find anything other than vending machine food. I thanked her and told her that I appreciated the offer but since I came in the hospital with no money, I was going to have to wait until I got home. But that was kind of silly anyways, because I just would have thrown it up after I ate it anyways. ☺

A side note here, the main way for me to maintain any kind of weight, since eating was almost impossible and frustrating with the nausea and loss of taste, I found that the vitamin/protein shakes that you can buy are quite good. *Only* the chocolate ones. That was the *only* flavor that tasted good (that I could actually *taste*) so I was buying them by the case! ☺

At around 10:30 PM I had just finished eating one of those little cereal boxes that you break open the box and pour milk in and then eat right out of the box (a nurse had "found" this in the staff fridge!). This consisted of cornflakes and skim milk from a little carton. I thought to myself that this wasn't going to upset *anything* but I had to have something in my stomach to keep it from growing like a big dog! (insert more humor here). It was after that much appreciated little box of cereal when the cute blonde physician came back in, with a cute little grin, told me that all the scans were *clear* and that is simply I was "very severely dehydrated." She said the juice that I had drank earlier did the trick but that I should drink at least 32 ounces more, of any juice I prefer, when I get home. I thanked her, I shook her cute little blonde hand and she said to have a good night and left the room. So it would seem that the day wasn't a total waste... after all, I got to see a cute blonde Doctor, yes? ☺

The nurse returned with discharge papers and she told me as long as I had completed treatment at the cancer center that I could go home. She showed me the quickest way to the hospital to get back to the cancer center where my car was parked so I wouldn't have to go through the whole parking lot that late at night. I left the ER and followed her directions and found my car without troubles. On my way home, I stopped and followed cute blonde doctor's recommendation and picked up 32 ounces of grape juice. By the time I got home I was somewhat relieved but still feeling like 100% crap and hoped I could sleep. I have to do it again in the morning.

Sleeping, during this chemo/radiation was problematic at best. It's difficult to sleep, or *attempt* to sleep, when all that can be felt is my body shaking almost uncontrollably, feeling so cold with several blankets, pain all over, *fear* ravaging my thoughts, a lot of tears...and not *knowing* how long this would last...or was I even going to *survive*? This was all new to me and all too real...and *surreal* as well.

*I need a hug...*

I think perhaps the most embarrassing moment came as I was leaving the infusion center. It was a particularly bad infusion, only meaning that the effects seemed much worse that day, I had tears in my eyes from the pain. Still wearing a surgical face mask, I walked past a nurse as I was leaving and she had asked me what was wrong. I told her it was just a bad day and I want to go home and try to forget about it. She attempted to lift my spirits a little by insisting that I remove my mask so she can see me smile before I left. As I pulled the mask down, parts that were left of my mustache came off with it. This *embarrassed me beyond belief*. The nurse could *immediately* tell and she gave me a hug and a smile she said "...with or without a mustache that I was still a handsome fellow". She wished me a good evening and I said the same and left.

I'm finding sometimes while writing this book that is difficult to try to explain or elaborate on everything that happens during these treatments. As my story is not typical, it is however, *similar* to other patients but just more *unique*. There were plenty of nice moments (after I was able to "settle in" and accept my treatments) like talking with other patients while getting chemo. Me being a clown that I am, I tried to make any patient that I talked to smile and maybe laugh if possible. Again, I did it simply because it made *me* feel good to try and help anybody out who was going through the same sometimes tortuous moments. It was something I felt I *needed* to do to take my mind away from what I was feeling and experiencing. Now this doesn't make me special, rather, it was just me being *me*!

At the end of my radiation/chemo treatment I went for a follow-up visit with my chemo Oncologist. The short and sweet of it is that he quite bluntly told me that I was *cancer free* and in *complete remission*! ☺ *Say that again, Doc?*

He said that the latest x-ray and lab reports indicated that there were no more active or live cancer cells and that the tumor had been reduced *significantly*, however, is still up to the surgeon to decide if it would be safe and effective to remove the tumor and any surrounding damaged tissue. I would have to wait a couple weeks for that decision.

*DID HE JUST SAY "CANCER FREE AND IN COMPLETE REMISSION?"* ☺

**1**"Take Another Look-
A Guide To Understanding Ourselves"     (Amazon.com

# Chapter 6

# The Third Wave

Surgery. More surgery. This time it's going to be a *big* one. This time they're going to *remove* the top half of my left lung (and Lord only knows what *else* they will find).

A few days before the actual surgery I went for a consult with surgeon. There, he was going to describe, in detail, the surgery he was about to perform and showed me exactly where the tumor was and he explained that he was going to make a large incision on the upper part of my back on the left side, approximately 18 to 20 inches in length shaped like a crescent. He would then remove the upper half of my left lung, several lymph nodes and any surrounding tissue that may have been damaged by either the tumor itself or the chemo/radiation treatments. As I suspected, he also advised me that he may or may not find *other problems*. He said he wouldn't know until he had me "opened up". Yeah, I really like hearing *this*. He then proceeded to advised me that the cancer I had was indeed located in a *dangerous spot*. He said because of my condition there is a good 10 to 20% chance that I *wouldn't* make it off the table! Furthermore, I would have a 1 in 3 chance of recurrence. *1 in 3?* I asked the surgeon if it would have any effect on my golf swing. He laughed and said "if you are a 'slicer' the surgery should correct that." We both laughed. I said on my follow-up visit I'll let him know how *that* works. As I was leaving his office the receptionist handed me yet *another* sheet of pre-op preparations and instructions.

On the way home, of course, all I could think about was the description the surgeon gave me of the surgery that *was* going to happen in *two days*.

The next two days I continued on as I have the last several weeks. The sickness, pain, nausea, no appetite and no sleep, as usual.

The day of the surgery I was to report to the hospital at 5:00 AM which I did. Since I knew I was going to be in the hospital for a few days I had a friend drive me there and came in with me prior to surgery, to give me some company and encouragement. As I followed the procedure of putting on a hospital gown and waiting in bed, lo and behold who would appear in my room but that wonderful Doctor with a German accent! He started right away speaking in German and I could pick up that he was wishing me a good morning and something else before I had to stop him and say "Auf English Herr Doktor, bite." Which is simply put means, "In English Doctor, please!" He laughed and proceeded to tell me how he attends two cancer seminars every month as well as specific classes relating to cancer and that he practices the latest therapies and in his opinion, the *best* cancer treatments. He assured me that he knew my *specific* type of cancer and *what* the tumor was *doing* and *where* was at, that I should be just fine after the surgery. He said of course there are going to be side effects from all the chemo/radiation and the surgery I was about to have. He said "your surgeon and your family Doctor will help you with those." He then shook my hand and again, in perfect German, he wished me good day and told me that things will turn out fine. I gave him a very sincere thank you and handshake and wished him the same. Not two or three minutes later a nurse came in the room and asked that my friend had to leave because it was time for me to go in for surgery. I could see the concern of my friends face as they left. This is a very scary feeling right now. I'm going in for surgery where the surgeon had given me *graphic* details about the surgery and me being somewhat artistic, I was visualizing this in my head. NOT a pretty sight!

I was wheeled into an operating room with several people standing around in full surgical garb making preparations and helping me onto the operating table. The anesthesiologist was injecting, once again, a sedative into the IV line that had been placed in my arm. And, once again, I was instructed to count backwards from 100. And, you guessed it; I only made it to 95.

As it turns out, the surgery, I'm told, lasted between 6 ½ hours to seven hours and since you're reading this now, I survived the operation! I was also told that the surgery consisted of: a "lobectomy" or the removal of the upper half of my left lung, removal of "suspicious" parts of my T2 through T4 vertebrae, a small portion of my number three rib and the removal of two lymph nodes.

What I can recall, I barely remember waking up in the ICU and I think I knew the friend that drove me to surgery was there. I do remember however, regaining consciousness long enough to realize I had made it through the surgery. The next thought I have is when I was being transferred from the ICU to my room. Two nurses helped me and the *many* tubes attached to me, to my bed. I know I did moan in great pain during the move and one nurse saying "that wasn't so bad now was it?" I didn't quite share her opinion, as I was on the *receiving* end. ☺

By the time I fully recovered from anesthetic I was able to comprehend fully where I was at and looked at my new home for the next few days. I saw a nice flat-panel TV on the wall directly in front of my bed. Behind me was a whole array of "medical looking stuff" with plugs and tubes attached to them. On my left was the bathroom and between me in the bathroom was what appeared to be a locked and automated dispensing device which turned out to be a morphine pump. I had two rather large, surgical-looking tubes going into my body on my left side through my ribs into my chest. I had an oxygen tube attached to my nose and had a large IV needle taped on my left arm. There were more tubes, but I will spare further detail on that! Suffice it to say I wasn't going *anywhere*. ☺

Later that same evening two friends came by for a short visit. I must confess that I was rather upset about the surprise visit because I had asked friends *not* to come see me for at least two days after the surgery. I just couldn't stand the thought of anybody seeing me like this. They stayed for short while and due to my having a lot of pain and being *very embarrassed* about anybody seeing me like this, they said good bye and left. After they left I attempted to sleep... but the nurses had other ideas. The nurses would come in quite regularly and quite often in the process making it impossible to sleep. As expected, the TV was short on variety as far as channels. But something is better than nothing...

One Doctor came in the following day and introduced himself as the brother of the surgeon performed surgery. I was a bit surprised because my surgeon was about 6'3" tall and his brother was about 5'8" tall. When I looked at him, with a puzzled look on my face, he proceeded to tell me that he "was the *good-looking* brother!" He informed me that my surgeon would be in to check on me in the next couple days and that he was busy, and asked him to check on me. My surgeon seemed "all business" whereas his brother was much more personable and friendly and I appreciated his humor. He said he had checked the nurse's reports and said that I was doing fine. He shook my hand and with a smile, he excused himself and left. I thanked him for his time and wished him a good day.

I have no appetite but I would really *like* to eat *something*. I know that sounds silly but that's how it was. The next day when food was actually brought to me it looked pretty good! A Philly cheese steak I think... which I never had the opportunity to eat *any* of it because I was hauled away for post-operative x-rays before I had a chance to take a bite. The good news though, that the kitchen was open to 11 PM and I was able to order a small portion of tuna salad that didn't taste too bad, all things considered, *hospital food*, but I could only take a few bites as I was feeling *quite* nauseous, lots of pain and no sleep. I really wanted that cheese steak though! ☺

*Briefly, this post-operative x-ray is a pain in my... EVERYWHERE!*

So, here I lay with tubes and needles sticking in me and so much commotion from nurses checking on me, adjusting my *tubes* and checking my incision, which was a new adventure in pain! My room was quite nice and I had it all to myself. It was a one-bed room and I was surprised that it wasn't a *two*-bed room. There was a unique and interesting feature about this room however, it appeared that there was a "recessed area" or "a notched in area" by the door that was designed to allow doctors and nurses to observe patients in two adjoining rooms simultaneously. The drawback to that was that at night even though the lights are out in my room, the light that shined in from this "observation notch" lit the room up like day and made it nearly impossible to sleep. Due to those pesky tubes again, and the nature of the incision on my back, I was not able to roll over on my side to shade myself from that light at night. Besides, it seemed that my doctors had set orders that I experience "absolutely no pain or discomfort *whatsoever*" which is the answer I got when I asked "why do the nurses come in every two hours and jabbed me in the stomach with a syringe full of painkillers when I have a monitored and locked morphine drip running?" The nurse simply explained that considering the surgery I just underwent, I was going to need those jabs. I asked if she could use the access port on my IV drip instead of stabbing me in the stomach and she replied "that's not how it's done". I figured the doctors and nurses knew what they were doing so I would just lay back and let them do it.

After three days I believe, right about the time I finished what little dinner I could eat when my stepson and his dad came in. Again, I was very glad to see both of them... just not like *this*! Even though my stepson had seen me going to the first round of chemo/radiation, it still made me uncomfortable. They both came in and sat down and asked about the surgery. I could only tell them what the nurses had told me. They both told me that their glad that the surgery is over and that I made it through. They asked me how long I would be in the hospital but I had no idea. After a little while my stepson and his father came over and patted me on the leg (as I was totally engulfed by TUBES) said goodbye and left. I was sad to see them go.

The following day I awoke to find my family doctor's partner in his practice had come to check in on me and see how I was doing. I let him know how glad I was see him and how much I appreciated him taking time to come and visit. He told me no worries that they both would often visit and check on patients if the other Doctor had an emergency where they couldn't come themselves. I thought that was a nice arrangement. He assured me that the surgery was a success and that I would be released within 7 to 10 days or when the post operative biopsies came back clean. He said he would fill my Doctor in on my condition, shook my hand and with a smile said goodbye and he left.

It seems that my dad had called the hospital the day of my surgery to find out how I was. He had called again the next day, to my room but I was unable to answer the phone and never even heard the phone ring. He called again the next day, as I knew he would, and I was able to answer the phone and had a nice talk with my dad. I told him that I was in good hands and that he, my mom and my brother shouldn't worry. He asked if there was anything I needed, I replied that I would love to have some of these tubes pulled out of me so I could use the bathroom! I explained the situation to my dad and with his infinite wisdom he replied "this too shall pass!" We both had a laugh although it *really* hurt for me to laugh! I was *very* glad he called. ☺

So, it looks like I'm going to be in here for a while...but there's one thing that is starting to concern me; I haven't gone to the *bathroom* in three days and I feel like I'm going to *explode* but I don't dare move, fearing I'll pull out, pinch or tangle some, if not all of these *damned tubes*. I did notice however, that the cup of ice water that is brought into me as each nurse starts their shift had this strangely familiar taste of that "magnesium citrate stuff" which told me that the doctors or nurses knew *something* had to be done to alleviate my discomfort! By the fourth day a surgeon who I was unfamiliar with, and attractive brunette by the way, came in to remove my chest tubes. That in itself was one more little surprise I had in store for me. And yes it *was very* painful. But, looking for the *positive* out of all of this, my appetite was returning at a nice pace, and I was starting to enjoy the food. Right now, even hospital food was tasting like haute cuisine! I wonder what Chef Gordon Ramsay would say about the cuisine? ☺

This morning turned out to be a very special day. Today, there was *one very specific* tube that I was going to have removed... this being a very good thing! Two very nice nurses came to my room and inform me of their intent on removing that *certain* tube. As this was going to be a "delicate procedure" I stated, for modesty's sake, that I would prefer to remove this tube myself. Much to my surprise, the tube *refused* to be extracted! At this point the nurses were actually laughing saying "good luck with that, Kev!" They then proceeded to deflate a small bladder that was (unknowingly to me) located in such a position that the tube could *not* be removed without deflation of that bladder. After the bladder was deflated, with nurses still grinning, they removed that *ridiculous* tube. I was now free and clear to navigate! They removed the automated morphine drip machine two days prior, which was the same day that I believe my chest tubes were removed, and I no longer had that *other* irritating contraption attached to my legs. To me, these are all *very* good signs.

The next day was pretty uneventful except for the now routine poking and prodding and jabbing my stomach with syringes, sleeping when I can when I'm not being carted off for some test or being checked by nurses. I was surprised to wake up to find these peculiar looking devices that were attached to my legs! They were inflating and deflating, on a regular basis...obviously to keep circulation going in my legs. (These damn things just *will not* let me sleep!) Wouldn't want a blood clot now would we? Actually, they were a precursor of what's to come! Yup...they are gonna want me to *walk* pretty soon! Yeah *right*! As *if*! Sure enough...day 5 was going to be fun.

A young man, from physical therapy came in to take me for a walk! Knowing I was going to have to do this eventually...*now* is the time! He strapped a belt around my waist (to help pick me up if I drop!) and he had a portable oxygen tank. He grabbed the IV stand and had me walk into the hallway. Walking into the hallway, a nurse was there and said "it's nice to see you up and about. How are you feeling?" I responded that I was feeling okay and I was not looking forward to venturing out of my room quite yet. I was walking quite slowly of course, the physical therapist was holding onto my IV stand, wheeling along with me and has other hand firmly grasping the belt placed around my waist and kept telling me that if I felt too winded, felt like passing out, lightheaded, or in too much pain to let him know and he would get me back to my room. I got to carry the oxygen tank! "Tanks a lot!" ☺

I was only able to make it about 20 or 30 feet if I remember correctly, when he said "I was starting to look pale" and put me in a wheelchair and got me back to bed. He hooked up everything he had unhooked for my "marathon" and put that device back on my legs and started them up again. He asked me how I was feeling and said I did very well all things considered, shook my hand and said he would see me tomorrow. I thanked him for his time and settled in to rest, watch a little TV, maybe eat a lil bit and try to sleep. As soon as I could catch my breath I called for room service! ☺

The following day was pretty much a carbon copy of the previous day. Poking, prodding, changing dressings, changing bed linen, physical therapy (I was able to walk almost twice as far today) and... *Interrupting* my much-needed *sleep*! Considering that I'm told I'm doing fine... I *still* need to use the *bathroom*!

Okay, today is the day! I'm going into the bathroom, being careful not to tangle any of my constant companions, the *tubes*... and make an *attempt* to get some *relief*! Rather than giving details here, I will simply say that due to my "strenuous efforts", the wireless monitor I had in my hospital gown must have alerted the nurses to my *predicament* as I was very surprised and taken aback by two big nurses rushing into my room and finding me in the bathroom! Needless to say I was *extremely* embarrassed to be seen in the position I was in. I assured the nurses that I was fine and asked for a little privacy! They both left, with a silly grin on their faces and I'm sure an amusing story to share with the rest of the nurses. A very short time later... I *knew* what childbirth was like! Needless to say, I was much more comfortable and jumped back into bed. A short time later my dad called again, I told him the story of the bathroom incident. He laughed out loud!

I'm always so glad to hear him laugh. Each time I go out to see my family on the weekends, I like to make my dad *laugh*. ☺

Today appears to be a red letter day. A couple friends stopped by to see how I was doing. As much as I appreciated my friends taking time for a visit, it would have been nice if I could have been better company, but as I was still quite "doped up" I found it difficult at best to communicate. I noticed that everyone who came to visit only stayed for short time and they seemed very uncomfortable being there. I'm sure it wasn't anything other than hospitals make many people *uncomfortable*. Knowing this, I didn't take it personally.

As I lay here, over these last few days, I seemed to be overwhelmed by loneliness. I guess that's just another after effect of everything I've been through over the course of the last several months. This SUCKS! At this point, I think a "two-bed room" would have been nice for company.

I believe that the fifth and sixth day were relatively uneventful save for the fact that I was actually now able to walk the entire length around my ward, without having to stop to catch my breath, and was actually even close to trying to go around once again. The physical therapist told me "don't push it" and I agreed.

On the seventh day my surgeon came in and informed me that all the biopsy reports have been completed. He reminded me of everything he did in the procedure and explained *what* they were looking for in each biopsy taken. He informed me that my progress after surgery was very good, and that he didn't foresee any further complications other than slightly diminished mobility in my left back due to the incision. He then informed me of the biopsy results. He said all biopsies came back *negative… not* meaning there was *no cancer* in the biopsies, rather that the biopsy showed no *living* cancer cells. And, his ultimate statement was that he affirmed his prognosis of "a *good recovery* but that I had *still* a *1 in 3* chance of *recurrence.*" Although that wasn't *exactly* what I wanted to hear, it was the truth and acceptable as pretty good odds. He then informed me that he wanted me to stay another day or so "for further observation."

Upon my release from the hospital after 8 days, it was nice to see daylight again! When I went in for surgery...I wasn't really *sure* if that would happen!

I didn't know *if* I would be going home...

The same friend, who took me in for surgery, picked me up and drove me home. The ride home this time of the hospital was *much* better.

I was actually feeling good and my doctor's prognosis gave me just a bit more hope.

*What I didn't know at the time was that the worst was yet to come.*

I'm home now and it's a very comforting feeling. Sweetie and Puddin (my two lil orange fur-babies!) ...were *very* glad to see that Papa was home! All is good and getting better!

The next few weeks are going to be tedious at best, because due to the nature of my surgery getting in and out of bed is next to impossible without assistance of some kind. As I found out the very first night at home, that the only non-painful, way to get out of bed (or into bed for that matter) was to roll out onto the floor, which had painful results! So, as my couch has a built-in recliner… this is where I would stay for the next few weeks at least. I prop pillows up on either side of myself and recline. I'm actually to sleep quite well there! Since I obviously was not going to be able to cook my own meals for a while I had to rely on those "nuke-n-puke- microwave- meals". They weren't too bad, although I prefer "home-cooked from scratch" of *course*. What actual food I *could* eat was fine and I supplemented eating with those "ensure" protein drinks. The *chocolate* ones! My taste and sense of smell have been returning over the last couple of weeks.

My hair has started to grow back by this time, and so now I look like a fuzzyheaded Uncle Fester! The only hair I had remaining after chemo/radiation treatments, were my eyebrows, *partially*! Will someone *please* explain *that* one? Well, at least while washing my hair won't be a problem since I have lots of body wash! ☺

My surgeon had prescribed "in-home nursing" where a nurse from the hospital would come by every other day and check the progress. There were three nurses assigned to me and they alternated their visits. These "home visits" would last for approximately 30 days, my case will be reviewed to see if further homecare was needed.

A week after I was released, my surgeon requested that I come into his office for a quick checkup. I had a very difficult time getting in and out of the car not mentioning trying to *drive* the car!

Just walking the short distance from the parking lot to the elevators, I was struggling to breathe! With the upper half of my left lung gone...it was very difficult at first adjusting to not being to be able to take a deep breath just to be able to relax!

On a side note, the funny thing about the lungs tho...and I *knew* this...the lung itself would "adjust and expand" *filling* the void left by surgery! I had always wondered what would be done about the *space* left where the top half of my lung was? Would my heart flop around too without the lung holding it in place? Silly I know, but these are *real* things I thought about! For the first 2 years or so afterwards, my doctors would "listen to my lungs during my checkups. They would listen to the *upper half* of my right lung, then the *lower half* of my right lung. Then they would listen to the *lower half* of my left lung...*but not the top!* When my doctors started listening to the "upper half" on the *left* side of my back, I could tell the lung had *expanded*!

Also during the first couple years...I could actually *feel* my left lung, or what's left of it, seem to "jump" if I coughed! A *very* uncomfortable feeling!

While meeting with the surgeon, he indicated that the nurse's reports so far were encouraging and he assured me how to feel a lot better in a few weeks. He also informed me that at a meeting at the board of surgeons reviewed my case. They did *not* recommend any further treatments or follow-up chemotherapy. However my hematology Oncologist recommended *another* round of chemotherapy. It would not be the five days a week over a period of a few months, rather, it would be one infusion every three weeks for 2 ½ months. The surgeon informed me that my Oncologist ordered this round to "just make sure" and so they could say "we've done all that we could do." NOT very comforting! The tone in his voice didn't appear to me, to be very optimistic. But I on the other hand, I'm all about *optimistic*. I thanked him for his candor. Then, knowing how I love the game of golf and knowing that I have been attempting to golf the whole while prior to surgery, he informed me that for the type of surgery he did to patients who golfed reported that their "slice" (when you drive the golf ball and it curves *right*, straight off the tee! NOT a good thing!), was all but eliminated! I thought to myself "COOL!"

Now that I was home, it was driving me *crazy* because it was so difficult to do anything that I normally did around the house. Laundry, cleaning, mowing the yard and even emptying litter boxes was very difficult due to the fact I couldn't bend over or lift anything and I was still a little too weak to venture downstairs to do laundry. At about two weeks after surgery and *not* being too happy about to sitting on my rear *and* not being able to do *anything*. I felt helpless and useless. So, I decided to attempt to do something that *desperately* needed doing... in my opinion anyways.

Since I had lost so much weight at the beginning of all the treatments (I went from 175 pounds to 135 pounds the first month) then ballooned up to 232 pounds! My God, NO!

Fact is, I actually had to go and buy "fat underwear"... when I got them home and held them up to see my new drawers I screamed "NOOOOOO!" These things looked *huge*! I tried them on and they fit *perfectly*! Since I did not really want to go out and buy new "fat" clothes, and needed to get off of the couch and do something... *anything*... to get rid of some of this fat that I had accumulated from the lack of activity over the last few months and perhaps drinking too many chocolate milkshakes! (I did say *chocolate*, yeah?) In my first attempt at actual activity, to try to get back the "normalcy" of my life, I put on an old pair of sweatpants, sweatshirt and shoes and went out to my garage. I was going to *mow my lawn*.

I went out to the garage and pulled the ol lawn mower out, primed the gas...and tried to get it started. This is where it gets interesting. Seeing that, since I just went through chemo/radiation *hell*, had the top half of my left lung removed, this may not be such a good idea! I attempted several times to start this mower...but quickly ran out of breath.

As I sat on my front porch, contemplating on "how" was I going to mow my lawn...and trying to catch my breath (after a few pulls on the lawn mower starter...c'mon, *really*?) I noticed one of my neighbors from down the street *running* over to my house! Not far behind her was her husband, pushing *his* lawn mower towards my house! When she got here, she immediately "let me have it" about trying to mow my lawn! (I was surprised that my "health troubles" reached that *far* down the block!) and ORDERED me to go inside and rest! *REALLY?!* Her husband proceeded to mow my lawn. It was at this moment, that I noticed two *more* neighbors were coming my way from the other side of the block, one had hedge trimmers in hand, while his "better half" scolded me too! A *CONSPIRACY!* ☺

Each neighbor then actually took me by my arms, guided me into the house and sat my behind on the couch and said, *almost in unison*, "SIT THERE AND REST! Don't worry; we'll take care of your lawn!" Well...I guess they told *me*, yeah? As much as I *truly appreciated* what they were doing...it was *uncomfortable* for me having others do my yard work. After the yard was done, they all came in and asked if I needed anything...well, I really was overwhelmed! As it turns out...I was correct! The neighbors I ran across during radiation treatments told a few neighbors (I told you we had a "close knit" neighborhood) and it spread down the street!

The next day, the same neighbor that ran down the street and ordered me into my own house, came by with a *hugh* bowl full of fresh fruit and other healthy goodies! Yeah, it did bring a tear to my eye...a happy tear though...it was so nice and *appreciated* to know my neighbors thought so much of me! And, not finished here, the next day, my *other* neighbor came by an asked if I needed anything from the store! I'm just not used to this! I mean, it doesn't surprise me...but still...

All the while I had been receiving TONS of cards wishing me well! Friends, neighbors AND total strangers! (I suspect my hair stylist put me on the "prayer list" at her church!)

My neighbor (with the fruit bowl) came by several more times to "check on me" and even offered to change the bandages and replace the 'fentynol patch'! I told her "Thank you" but I have nurses coming by and they take care of that!

Three weeks or so after being released from the hospital, I received a phone call from my Oncologist office. I was informed that I was to begin the *second round of chemotherapy* the following Monday. I was told I would follow the same procedure as before (minus radiation!) With regards to the infusions and that they would be one 5 ½ hour infusion every three weeks for approximately 2 ½ months. Since I still had the Mediport in me, at least that's *one thing* I didn't have to face again (except for the removal of the "port").That's "why" it wasn't removed...*sneaky*...

*Another round of chemo? Well, I was warned.*

I was just *starting* to feel a *little bit* back to normal, all things considered, and now my mind was filled with the memories of the *first round* of chemo. Sure, I didn't have to have radiation along with the chemo and it *was* only one day every three weeks...

*I was in for a real surprise.*

# Chapter 7

# The Final Wave

*More chemo*. My hair *just* started to grow back, the pain was *just* beginning to subside, my appetite was *just* starting to come back and I have *more* chemo.

Over the past few months, since the end of the first round of chemo and due to the fact that everything has knocked me on my butt, I seemed to have put on the weight I had lost... and then some. I can only figure out that with my appetite returning and drinking lots of *chocolate* milkshakes (for protein) I have *ballooned* to over 200 pounds (232 to be *exact!*) So I was hoping for a *positive* to happen during the second round of chemo where I could *lose a few pounds* and at least *start* to look *human* again. The first round of chemo quite literally drained all energy for me and the surgery afterwards proved to *immobilize* me even further... this is why I put on so much weight. However once all this is done and over with I can get out and *golf* and lose some of this lard! ☺

Although I knew the majority of the chemo drugs used in my *first round* were called "Cisplatin" (who the *hell* thinks of these *names*? I mean, let's call them what they *are*; POISON 1A, POISON 2314, etc?) C'mon now... "Cisplatin?" As it turns out my new "chemo-of-choice" was called "Taxotere". And wouldn't you know, this *stuff* was by far *worse* than the Cisplatin!

While driving to the infusion, the questions that were coming up were "what's this *crap* going to be like?" and "what's this *crap* going to do to me?"

I was going to find out soon enough, because I'm pulling into the parking lot now.

I walked into the infusion center and followed the same routine. I checked in, found myself a chair and sat down. I was shaking as the *fear* of the unknown aspects of this *new chemo* started once again. Two nurses came up to me and one asked for my name and date of birth, while the other nurse started to hang the IV bags with that *"suspicious lil red foil sticker"* on it, and without hesitation proceeded to plug my port into the chemo delivery machine (for lack of its *actual* name). Please believe that when I tell you that I could feel *this* "stuff" actually coursing through my veins *within a couple of minutes* of the nurse turning on the machine that was pumping the chemo into me.

This is getting scary quick. The first chemo didn't feel like this, nor did *any* of the chemo's during the first "pre-op chemo" round. This was an entirely *different* chemo and it seemed to get *worse* every minute as the 5 ½ hours passed.

The first hour was very uncomfortable from the *inside* and as it progressed into the second hour, it got worse in a very noticeable way. At first it was just making me feel "uncomfortably tingly" through my arteries and veins. As the chemo worked its way through my body the sensation felt more like a mild acid was being pumped in. it really felt like it was *burning from the inside out*! And this was only the second hour, of the first 5 ½ hour infusion and I had more to look forward to over the next 2 ½ months. By the end of the first infusion I honestly felt that I was being poisoned! I mean how can this do me *any* good when it's this *bad*, <u>so *soon*</u>. My body was experiencing same effects as the first round of chemo only much, *much* worse. What this "Taxotier" was doing to me is almost indescribable and very *unbelievably unbearable!* You *know* it's going to be *bad* from the start of the first (and *every*) infusion.

By the end of this first infusion, the same nurse that plugged me into this *wonderful* machine, came back to remove me from it. She asked me how I was feeling and I asked her "why?" She replied that I looked very pale and when she touched my skin around the port she commented that my body temperature was down and that I actually felt cold to the touch. She asked me how I was feeling and I tried to explain, to the best of my ability at that point, exactly how I felt. She told me that she was sorry that it (the chemo) was causing me so much "discomfort" and that it should pass within a few days. I knew she was trying to be comforting and reassuring but when she said "discomfort" I wanted to say "discomfort my ass! *You* plug yourself in and see if it's a "discomfort". Of course I didn't *say* that, I just find it sort of amusing how doctors and nurses refer to pain, nausea and vomiting as "discomfort"!

She cleaned up my port and put a fresh cover over it and asked if I had anybody there to drive me home. I told her no, that I had drove myself for the previous infusions and figured I could handle it this time as well. She asked me if I was up to driving and that if I wasn't feeling well enough to drive that she could arrange to get me a ride home. I told her I didn't want to leave my car in the parking lot overnight and I had no way of coming back to get it other than to take a taxi. I assured her that if at some point during my drive home that I didn't feel I *could* make it safely, that I would pull over and call 911. It was only a less than a 10 minute drive, no worries. She then handed me the usual "Post infusion" instructions and said I was free to go. She reminded me of the three-week appointment, told me to drive careful and to have a good night. I left the infusion center.

The drive home was uneventful except that the *effects* were increasing. I was hoping I could make it home.

By the time I got home this sheer *pain* that seem to occupy every square inch of my body, my skin and bones... *everything*, was getting *worse*. Halfway to my back door I collapsed on my knees and attempted to vomit. But I couldn't. My body was _screaming_ at me to "puke" and this just served to _intensify_ the pain!

After perhaps 5-10 minutes of desperately trying to throw up, I managed to make it into the house, get into my jammies and went to bed and tried to sleep.

As it turns out, this was going to be my _new_ routine for the next couple of months or so.

Both of my doctors, my family Doctor and my Oncologist, wanted me to try _marijuana_ in a "medicinal way" to help alleviate my pain, nausea, loss of appetite and sleeplessness. (my oncologist had _urged_ me to do this from the very start of treatments). It was at this time I decided to investigate "alternative methods" and "alternative cancer treatments". Now, mind you, I had smoked marijuana over 30 years ago (_recreationally_, of course, in high school) and hadn't given it much thought since. To be quite honest, however, if I had been someplace where somebody was smoking pot, sure, if I was offered, I would take a couple hits. That was about it. Now my Doctor is _recommending_ that I try marijuana _for the medicinal properties_ it had. I had a friend locate some "pot" and sure enough I was able to _replace_ four different _prescription medications_ (which were artificial and synthetic compounds as compared to the "_natural_ properties" of marijuana), this was a _no-brainer_ for me. Both my family Doctor and my Oncologist supported the use of "medicinal marijuana" and would be more than happy to help me get a "Michigan Medical Marijuana Registry Card" which would allow me to *legally possess* and *use* marijuana on the *medicinal* basis, following state law. (The State of Michigan passed a "medical marijuana Law" which took effect January 2009.)

I was also thinking about what the surgeon said about me having a *1 in 3* chance of recurrence. I knew in my heart that I didn't think I could make it if I had to go through all of this all over again... or *worse*.

When you're diagnosed with cancer, *any* stage of cancer, you start to ask *questions* and look for *answers*. As for myself, well, I wanted to get as much information as I could to see what I can do to *prevent* cancer from recurring and having to do all of these *hellish treatments* again.

I started to do research online by finding five or six books on the subject. I purchased six "alternative cancer treatment books" and read each one *quite carefully* taking note of *specific* "treatments/cures". I made a list of specifics that were found common in each book, although none of books were related to, linked to or affiliated with or *recommending* one another. I wanted *separate* and *individual resources that do not influence one another*. After this I took my list and conducted my own research. I was absolutely *amazed* at the results! I even went as far as to *verify* the *credentials* of specific *doctors* and resources for alternative treatments.

Each physician I researched came through with flying colors, as *"board certified"* and *"in good standing"* physicians. I also investigated the resources for vitamins, minerals, organic substances, etc. and was equally amazed.

Out of the six books that I researched one book stood out from the rest. It had more verified information and more detailed reports as well as *excellent* referencing and was written in a very "non-clinical" way.

The book that I *researched* and was *convinced* had the *most verifiable, useful and informative information* was a book by Ty Bollinger, who is now a good friend of mine. His book is called "<u>CANCER: Step Outside the Box</u>". And for the *record*, I *do not* and *would not accept anything* (meaning I was NEVER offered OR accepted *any* compensation) for mentioning this book. I recommend this book simply because the information within is *real* and verifiable and *truthful*. In fact, I actually asked permission from Ty to include *his book* in *my book*. He said he would be honored! Oh, did I mention that it was Ty who suggested and *encouraged* me to write this book?

Well he *did* and when a "bestselling author" encourages you to *write* a book, you *write a book*!

When Ty was writing his latest book, he wanted to include "cancer survivor" success stories. He had contacted me to ask permission to use my story in his new book. He provided a manuscript for my approval. I was extremely honored, that out of the *thousands* of people Ty's work has helped, that he chose *me* and *my story*. When I questioned him about that he simply said that my enthusiasm for helping other *people* and other *patients* is remarkable! I want to share your story, with your incredible and undeniable positive attitude towards battling cancer and living life, to others for *inspiration* and *encouragement*."

This totally floored me and as I told Ty, "Hey, I'm just doing what I can to help others because after all isn't that why we are here? Isn't that the way life *should* be?" I also asked him where he got this "humbling opinion" of me. He reminded me that we had exchanged signed copies of our books and that he learned a lot about me and "what kind of a man I am" through my book. That is one *hell* of a complement I felt *extremely* honored!

So like I said, when a *best-selling author suggests and encourages you* to write a book, *you write a book.*

It was Ty's suggestion that I *specifically* write, in as much detail as possible, my story as a cancer survivor to give *encouragement* and *hope* to both patients and survivors and their families and loved ones.

As I write this book and recall the events leading up to the writing of this book, I truly believe that the research I did lead me to an "alternative method/treatment" that has me healthy and helps me to get stronger every day. (details below)

Another side note here, when I first began the second round of chemo I had asked my doctor what he thought about two specific supplements that I wanted to take to help keep me from having a recurrence. He gave me a peculiar look and with a "tongue-in-cheek-response" he said "go ahead."

Now, not too long after the second surgery, I started to take several vitamins, supplements and was being careful about what I ate. I stay away from "fast food" (this is hard...but, I reward myself once in a while with *maybe* a couple taco's or have a nice cheeseburger) and I was avoiding sugar as much as possible (cancer cells *seem* to love sugar) and I got as much exercise as possible. Walking and golf were the main activities.

Through my research on methods and treatments for *prevention* of cancer or "recurrence", the following list details what I found that I was going to utilize to keep cancer away and help my body recover.

As I have researched *each item*, I found that they *all* were natural, *very* inexpensive and had *many benefits*. The more I researched, I was amazed at how these simple vitamins and supplements aid our bodies in so many ways. As I discovered, one single "dose" of chemo cost about $3800.00 PER DOSE!

Then, comparing the total cost for the vitamins and supplements, this was yet another "no brainer"!

Through a couple *very reliable* on-line resources (swansonvitamins.com), I was able to get a year's worth of these vitamins and supplements for just under $200! All were 'all natural', all were of very high quality and reliability AND are having positive and documented positive effects on *me*! I feel *really* good, all things considered! ☺

My doctor and oncologist recommend some (if not all) to their patients!

The following "regimen" that I follow to this day is *very* inexpensive and since I researched these vitamins and supplements *myself*...I am *positive* and *believe* in them *completely* and I would *recommend* others to "research" for themselves!

Remember, *truth* is *knowledge*...knowledge leads to *understanding* and understanding gives us *acceptance*.

The daily "regimen" I am following is as follows:

- B17-100mg/daily (apricotpower.com)

- B12-100mg/2x daily (pharmacy)

- B6-100mg/2x daily (pharmacy)

- D3-2000iu's/daily (pharmacy)

- Omega 3-1000iu's/daily (pharmacy)

- Lutein-20mg/daily (pharmacy)

- Glutamine-500mg/daily

(swansonvitamins.com

- Glutathione-100mg/daily
(swansonvitamins.com)

- Zinc-50mg/daily (pharmacy)

Now, as this all seems like a lot, but remember, most of these are sold in quantities of 100 per bottle (which at one a day, that's about 3 ½ month's supply in each bottle!) So the cost for *prevention* and *better health* is roughly $40 a month! And on top of that, *both* my doctor *and* oncologist *fully agree and support my research and in my taking these vitamins and supplements <u>and</u> benefits they provide!*

Now here's where it gets *interesting*. Towards the end of my second round of chemo I was informed that my Oncologist was leaving this particular cancer center because he was offered a position at *another* cancer center as "Director of Research/Oncology". However he was *still* going to see patients and informed the nurse that he wanted to continue my care himself. So for following progress checkups I followed him to the new cancer center. (More on that in the following chapter.)

To continue, these once every three week infusions were *incredibly* hard on me both in *body* and *mind*. The symptoms I described on the initial day of the second round *intensified* beyond belief. These effects didn't last for just a few days rather; they lasted for over two weeks and they would only *start* to subside within a couple of days of the *next infusion*.

This made it extremely difficult when I went for the next infusion because I *knew* what the previous infusions had done and it's just going to happen all over again for several more weeks. Looking for the *positive* though, I was looking forward to losing some of the fat gained! This was not to be. Just as before, the chemo stripped me of my sense of taste and smell and appetite. The only thing I could eat and actually *taste*, were *chocolate* milkshakes… again! This would prove to be yet another "weight adding" experience. I asked my Oncologist what I should do at this point. He smiled and told me that the weight gain was due to my body being saturated with the chemo drugs. During this time my metabolic rate was slowed down to a crawl. Even if I *were* to exercise daily during the chemo (yeah *right*, I don't even have the strength to blink my eyes alone exercise!), my metabolism *wasn't working* and I would not be able to lose any weight and this round left me *completely drained* of all energy. He also informed me that after treatments were completed, that it could take as much as 18 months to *two years* for my body to *"reboot"* from all that it has gone through. So it was going to take *up to two years* to *start* feeling "normal" again? This SUCKS…but it is what it *is*, I guess.

*Knowing* what was to come during and after this *hopefully* last round of chemo, I set my determination level to "high". At this point I'm determined to get through this and *focus* on the *positive* things that lie ahead… like helping my family, helping my senior neighbors, golfing, doing my yard work *myself* and losing all of this "chemo fat" as I call it and getting back to *living* and *enjoying* life.

However, this is going to have to wait…for now. I still have to get thru the final chemo assault. I was taking several vitamins and supplements and my research was continuing to reaffirm my initial research results. What's more, I was living *proof* that what I was doing *works*!

The second round was leaving me so weak and tired…and with a lot of *pain* in my joints, muscles and skin were still leaving me somewhat incapacitated…something I *couldn't* adjust to! I remained as positive as I could…and *believed*.

However...all those vitamins and supplements *were actually helping me!*

I could *feel* and *see* the benefits! Also, my research actually showed how Glutamine and Glutathione were beneficial for patients who were getting "Cisplatin"!

*The "torture" from chemo would end soon.*

*PLEASE NOTE:*

*Consult your family doctor before using ANY vitamins or supplements! I am NOT a physician and I am only describing how these vitamins and supplements help ME!*

*Please refer to page 165 for more info.*

# Chapter 8

# Follow-ups

It's been just about 2 ½ months, the second round of chemo is completed. As I said before, everything that happened during the first round happened again in the second round… only way more *severe*.

On the last day, of the last infusion, I was instructed to call my Oncologist for a follow-up visit in two weeks. Thereafter, for the next *two years* I would be having follow-up visits with my Oncologist every three months. I called my Oncologists office and the receptionist and informed me that they had already scheduled an appointment for me in two weeks time.

This was going to be a nerve racking. As I was investigating cancers and treatments I found that if a *"recurrence"* of cancer was going to happen it statistically happens within the first 18 months to two years *after* treatment (my oncologist *confirmed* this on my 3½ year check-up). For instance, the actress Farrah Fawcett had gone through aggressive cancer treatments and remained in remission for almost a year, then her cancer *returned* with a *vengeance*. Sadly, she passed away within months of the recurrence. Not long after her passing, actor Patrick Swayze was also diagnosed, aggressively treated and in remission for almost 9 months. His cancer returned and took him within months of the recurrence.

These facts were *not* very comforting to me as my *initial* cancer diagnosis was as severe as theirs, so going for follow-up visits at three month intervals, made me nervous and each time I would go I would have a chest x-ray prior to the appointment and blood drawn the day of the appointment. The results of these tests would be reviewed by my Oncologist and the results would be given to me at each subsequent visit.

The initial post-treatment follow-up was good only in the fact that my Oncologist told me that all tests, reports and exams to date were *very* promising. Also at this first visit, since I had not seen my Oncologist since he was at the other cancer center, the first thing he said was that I was looking good and that he was going to keep a close eye on my case so I shouldn't worry. He also told me that for the next two years I was to relax and *enjoy life*. I told him that was going to be hard to do since I felt like I weighed as a baby elephant! He laughed and assured me that it was normal considering what I have just gone through.

Then, by complete surprise, he asked me about the "alternative treatments" I had investigated and wanted to know about all of these supplements, minerals and vitamins that I was taking. When I asked him why, all of a sudden, he was *interested* in these things but at the other cancer center he would barely comment on it. His response was "I was *contractually bound* to *not* discuss or recommend *any* other form of treatment other than the traditional methods (chemo, radiation and surgery)". He said "Now that I am *here* (at a new cancer center) and I am the *"Director of Research"* I want to *know* and *do* anything possible to help patients survive cancer and live a long, healthy and happy life." He then asked me to list *in detail* everything I was doing. He said he wants to monitor me and see the progress. It was about this time when I had informed him about my research into "alternative treatments" and the results I came up with. As I discussed my newfound knowledge regarding how cancer cells work, how our bodies react and defend against cancer, etc. and the *natural substances* that I have found that have been *clinically proven effective* in *treating, preventing and curing cancer.* the more I told him, the more wider his eyes got! He said "my, you *have* been doing some research... and you are *absolutely correct* in what you have found in regarding to how cancer cells work, how they develop and how effective natural occurring vitamins, supplements and minerals work to fight cancer." With that, I thanked him for getting me through this and appreciated his candor while discussing alternative means to preventing and fighting cancer. He mentioned he was glad to see one of his patients becoming so pro-active and *not* succumbing to their fate while dealing with a cancer diagnosis. As he has read my first book, he said he would like to tell other patients of my case and positive attitude I displayed during all of the treatments.

In the three months since the visit with my Oncologist, I have been trying to get back my life as much as possible.

About a month after treatment was finished, I was still dealing with a lot of *pain* and the *nerve damage* to my hearing due to the chemo, made it hard to go out in public because my hearing *acuity* was so *increased* I could hear a fly fart from across the room! ☺ Since it has been almost 11 months since I have been able to go out to my parents and make them dinner it was right around Thanksgiving and of course I was going to be bringing and cooking a full course, traditional Thanksgiving dinner with *all* the trimmings for my dad, mom and brother. I had a lot to be thankful for, yeah?

I was feeling *much* better as it would turn out, the snow once again started to fly and accumulate here in Michigan. The time is now to go out and crank up my snow blower. Now I wasn't worried about being cold because I had so much *fat* on me that it insulated me quite well from the cold. However hauling around all that extra lard made *everything* more difficult and I was runnin on just 1½ lungs! But I was determined not to let my seniors and my neighbors down. They were there for me as much as they could be and I *appreciated every effort* they made for me. So now it's *my* turn to return *their* kindness. Like I said in my first book: "Kindness is its own reward. Kindness *returned* is a bonus!"

This was about the same time that I started to realize what some of the side effects from chemo/radiation/surgery and *more* chemo would be.

One of the first things I noticed was that in colder weather my left hand appeared to be colder to the touch than my right hand. Also, I had noticed that I seem to perspire *more* on my right side and *less* on my left side during strenuous activities.

It would seem that since none of my doctors had mentioned any other side effects that were caused by the surgery and minimally from the chemo/radiation, as each cancer case is different, the extent of what "damage" was caused are still to be discovered. So far the biggest problem or *side effect* from *everything* so far would be enormous and unprecedented *weight* gain! I have never had this much extra weight and I felt *grotesque* in my appearance alone, not to mention the difficulties in doing day to day activities with all this extra weight. Just getting out of bed in the morning was a *humiliating* experience for me.

The next obvious side effects were the damage to one of my "optic nerves", the rather large, painful scar on my back and the arthritis in my left shoulder and hip. I think the extent of the neurological damage is known and I have accepted it and can deal with it.

I consider these "battle scars" and have *accepted* them and *learned* to *deal* with them.

So it would go for the next two years that every three months was going to be a wait-and-see scenario, while trying to get back to some sense of "normal" in my life.

And I was determined to remain *hopeful* and *positive*. ☺ I was still *scared as hell* before each follow-up...

For the next two years, every three months I would go to see my oncologist. Every time he would come into the exam room he would say with a smile, "Hi Kev! How are you today?" To which my *usual* response was "I don't know Doc, you tell *me*"... Whereas he would just smile and tell me everything's perfect. He would continue to inquire about my "alternative methods" that I was doing to stave off a recurrence. With each visit to his office he was more and more interested in what these "methods" were doing. He encouraged me to "just keep doing what you're doing" and assured me that I was going to do just fine. He also asked me about my golf game and if I was getting out to golf. *Silly question!* ☺

After treatments were completed I thought it would be a good idea for me to do something nice for myself. So at approximately 4 months after treatment, I went to visit my best friend and his family in Arizona and *golf like maniacs* for a few days to celebrate my friend's birthday. That trip was *just* what the doctor ordered! For the first time in my life, for some strange and unexplainable reason, I actually didn't mind the four hour flight! (I really don't like to fly! When I do, I usually fly *XANAX airlines*!) ☺

I had such a wonderful time visiting with my friend and his family and golfing at several very nice golf courses with my friend, when I came back to Michigan, although it was late February and very cold, I came back with the warmth of spending time with my friend and his family. I can't wait for my friend come back to Michigan so we can do some *serious* fishing! I like catching 28 inch rainbow trout! (He'll *know* what I mean!) ☺

A couple months after I came home from my much needed "get away"...more bad news. My mom's health takes a turn for the worse.

Sadly, my mom was diagnosed with "endometrial carcinoma" in 2008. Her doctor had cleared her for surgery to remove the cancerous tissue and even stated that she wouldn't need any chemo or radiation. She could be completely cured with a somewhat minor operation. I say "somewhat" because my mom wasn't in the best of health anyways and being a senior citizen in her mid-80s surgery would be more risky for her than it would have been for someone younger. Yet, her doctor had in fact cleared her for surgery and assured her that she would recover just fine. It was four months after my mom's diagnosis in 2008, that I was diagnosed in 2009. My mom refused any and all treatments that were suggested and *encouraged* by her doctor.

While I was undergoing treatment I would talk to my dad about my mom's condition and tried to encourage him to just get her to the hospital and have it done. My mother was pretty much wheelchair bound at this point so she would have been a "captive audience". The problem at hand with that, would be that my mother would *not* want to do any of the post operative exercises and routines that would help her heal faster. I tried telling my dad that mom needed to do something *immediately* because there is no way she would tolerate or even just *survive* for that matter, chemotherapy and/or radiation. My mother's cancer finally took her on Memorial Day 2010. I had seen her at the hospital just a few hours before she had passed. My dad went to feed her lunch and asked if I would go feed her dinner (she was pretty much totally blind by now).When I got to the hospital to visit her I had talked to the attending physician taking care of mom. He basically told me that her tumor was bleeding out and there was nothing more they could do.

I went in to see my mom sitting in a chair sweating profusely and they were giving her blood. LOTS of blood! The nurse had informed me that she was on the fourth bag of blood! When that bag had emptied they had cleaned mom up and put her back to bed. It was obvious she was suffering and there was *nothing* I could do. Her dinner had just arrived and I asked her if she wanted something to eat, she said no, that she just wanted to sleep. So I leaned over and I gave her a hug and told her that I loved her. She said "I love you" then closed her eyes and slept. At this point her family Doctor entered her room and motioned for me to step out of the room. He had known the whole time what I was going through and assured me repeatedly that he was constantly trying to get my mother to accept some form treatment for her cancer. He even suggested that she use some of the same methods I was using such as vitamin B-17 and vitamin D3, but she refused. I could see it in his eyes that mom *wasn't* going to come home that night. He told me they're going to try and stabilize her and make her as comfortable as possible. I thanked the doctor for his time and let him know how much I appreciated everything he's done for my mom and dad and brother over the last 15 years or so. He shook my hand and asked me to give his regards to my dad and brother. That was the last time anyone in my family would see my mom alive. She died at 3:17 AM the next morning.

I don't understand fully why my mom decided *not* to fight cancer. It was easily *treatable* and totally *curable*. It makes no sense. I find it hard to understand why *anybody* would *refuse* treatment no matter what stage the cancer may be at. It makes me think back to when I first met Howard in the radiation Department. As much as I understood his *fear,* I had hoped for and actually saw Howard's *fear* change to a more *optimistic* outlook towards the last time that I saw him. It was so cool to see how he seemed to be getting more *positive* and *upbeat* every day by just a few words from another patient.

The rest of 2010 was hard but it was getting better every day. Although my body and mind were still recovering from all that I went through in 2009, I was trying to put that all behind me concentrate more on my family, my cats, and golf.

So, this is the way, I thought, I was going to at least *try* to live my life as *happy* and *stress-free* as possible. I focused on my family and enjoying life. Needless to say I was *golfing* whenever possible and would golf with *anybody* whether they were good or bad it didn't matter as long as we had *fun* on the course. I still *sucked* playing golf, but I *was* getting *better.*

On the two-year anniversary of me being "cancer free" I was feeling pretty darn good. I was still having a hell of a time losing the weight but both of my doctors were very encouraging and optimistic. They both had told me that once my body had "healed" that the weight wouldn't be a problem.

Also on my second year remission anniversary, my oncologist surprised me by telling me that the National Cancer Institute had conducted studies on "alternative cures/treatments" and determined that the claims for vitamin B 17 (derived from apricot pits, *naturally*) and vitamin D3 (also a natural derivative) that they can *both prevent and cure cancer* were in fact, *valid!* This blew my mind! My oncologist, being the Director of Research Oncology telling me this is *incredible*.

Then we discussed the "odds" that I was given after treatments. Remember, "1 in 3"! I had mentioned to my oncologist where I have researched and found that the farther away you get from treatment and are in *remission*, the better your chances are of *actually surviving*. He agreed. I also mentioned that I had researched my specific form of cancer (with its complications) on WebMD what I found there was that somebody with a very similar diagnosis was only given "a 10% chance of making it to the five year mark". Both my family Doctor and my oncologist were quite *pissed* off at the information that WebMD was putting out! They both informed me that "each and every cancer diagnosis is *different*". Furthermore, they were *both* convinced that WebMD only reported the most serious outcome for *any* diagnosis. They *both* told me that I had *beat* WebMD's "estimate or prediction" and that I was to continue to just keep doing what I'm doing. Enjoy and live life... and keep working on my golf swing! ☺

Whereas "WebMD" can provide information, they usually provide the "worse case example" for conditions or illnesses. People should NOT presume that a "WebMD diagnosis" (from searching 'symptoms' on the site) is accurate and applies to themselves!

ALWAYS CONSULT YOUR FAMILY DOCTOR FOR ANY HEALTH CONCERNS! OR CALL 911 FOR EMERGENCIES! ☺

# Chapter 9

# Crossroads

For as much as I felt so alone, so lonely going through cancer treatment on my own, the thought of trying to find "that someone special" crossed my mind many times. In fact by the end of 2011 I had given it long and hard thought while trying to find someone. The main concern that kept popping up most was that, being the kind of man that I am and not wanting to burden anybody with my troubles, I felt that perhaps I should just *accept* the fact that I *couldn't* do that to somebody, to burden them with my troubles. The *truth* was that I had some physical and neurological damage caused by cancer itself, the chemo, radiation and the surgery and having a hard time myself dealing with it, I couldn't ask or expect someone else to deal with it as well. So once I faced the *truth* about the after effects, I pretty much *accepted* that *understood* how my life would be from that point on. And...I was fine with it.

*I accepted things the way I saw them.*

In retrospect, however...there were other "crossroads" I encountered.

During the initial "treatments"...the "emotional changes" *that happen to every cancer patient*, started to intensify. There were no "emotional 'highs' though. ...just the "lows"...

When the word 'cancer' is in *your* life as a patient, it is most difficult to see *any*thing except the reality of what your body...and mind are going through.

And as much as I *despise* the thought of "suicide" (I feel suicide is 'selfish', as one's suffering may be over, it creates *more* suffering for those who cared and loved the one who is now gone. Make sense? It's just *my* opine on that subject.)

However...having a *toxic chemical* pumped into your body, combined with *many* "doses" of radiation...AND...the pure *fear* of suffering the "effects" and possibly *dying* from the "treatment"...or the cancer tumor itself may end my life...again, I had *brief thoughts* of "ending my suffering"...I just feel I would have been *selfish* of me and, quite honestly...I don't have the "stones" to do it!

*I must admit...that there were a couple times...where I seriously considered ending my life with a 9mm bullet to my head. As most serious and disturbing that may sound, and totally against my beliefs about suicide...I did give it serious thought!*

You would have to *experience for yourself* the effects of *massive chemotherapy and radiation* as described earlier to *truly know and understand* the "why" and "how could I even think that" aspect of cancer treatments.

During the chemo/radiation "treatments" there was a common and terrifying thought I had almost every day thru out all treatments...was "will I wake up in the morning?"

This was the question that went thru my mind as I went to bed each night. Recalling stories and accounts I have read of having a chemo infusion one day...and not waking up the next day! And also seeing reports whereas approximately 75% of "cancer deaths" it wasn't the cancer that caused death. It was the CHEMO! As I could feel chemo and the effects, with every "something" that came up, an unexpected pain, behavioral changes, neuro/physical changes, etc, all would bring up the "silent specter" of "will *this* be *the* dose that *gets me*?" it was a question that kept answering itself with "not yet!"

Each day that I woke, I was glad, of *course*, that I was *still alive*...but...as with most days during 2009, I knew I had to face it all over again. And to this very day, I can't figure out HOW I got thru all of it?

Most, but not all, cancer patients and survivors I have talked with say they have had similar thoughts during the rough parts (hint: it was ALL rough parts!) BUT...they, as I, found the one reason to NOT "end it all"! Yes...everything associated with chemotherapy, in my experience anyway, is simply put, *devastatingly* horrible. A fate I couldn't wish on the worst of humans.

But, each day I woke up and managed to go back to the cancer center...every day...as much as I couldn't tolerate the pain and the feeling of my body struggling to survive during this "chemical attack"...as much as I seriously thought I need to stop this...NOW...I kept going back. I never brought out my gun or even looked at it (I only had it because a golf buddy on the police force wanted me to be able to protect myself during treatments and recovering. He also gave me safety info and arraigned for me to obtain a "Concealed Pistol License". So, it sits in my home in a secure place. It's for home protection. And it's my 2nd amendment right!

So, I came across yet another crossroad...made a decision and followed my path! So far it looks like I made a good choice! ☺

I took my oncologists advice to heart, meaning, he told me to "enjoy and live life". That's what I *intended* on doing. The second-year follow-ups presented *crossroads* for me in my mind and in my soul. *Crossroads* can be *very* important to a person because they can direct you on a *good path* or a *bad* one. The *trick* is to look at the crossroad with a *positive* mind, a *kind* heart and a *gentle* soul, *and* if you put 100% into *any positive effort* in your life you *will* get 100% positive in return! Well, this is how *I* like to live my life and it *works* for me.


*We all face crossroads every day and what we do at these crossroads determines how our lives will go.*

That's how I approached each follow-up during the second-year. I approached the *crossroad* between "uncertainty and fear" and "positive thinking and healthy life", well, I chose the latter. I was *not* going to allow negativity, uncertainty and fear into my life. I *sought out and focused* on as much *positive* as I could find and *found that there is comfort in the truth which leads to knowledge, then understanding and acceptance* and that a *positive way of life is better than the alternative.* Furthermore, if I know someone, or meet someone who is having difficulty with the "negatives" that life sometimes brings, I will offer a kind word, positive thought or even a hug if needed. Sometimes even the simplest acts of *kindness* have *profound and positive results.* IT'S TRUE! ☺

And whereas I understand that not EVERY act of kindness or offer of help may or may not be appreciated (or at least acknowledged) …the immediate effect is INSIDE US when we DO something nice or help others.

I went into each follow-up exam in the second-year the *positive and optimistic attitude.* My oncologist and the nurses in the office couldn't believe it! The doctor and I both left the exam room together one day and I shook his hand and thanked him as he then informed me that I would only have to come back every *four months* for my third year. I stood there for a second, just absorbing what he just said and smiled. I overheard him say as he was walking into the next exam room and his next patient, "...there goes another success story. He's a *real survivor!*" (He was pointing at me, over his shoulder with his thumb as he said this, while closing the door to see his next patient!) And that just made me *smile* that much more! ☺

Still, with all the *good*, and all of the *positive* I have found and embraced, I still had a hole in my heart. There was also a piece of my *soul* that seemed to be *missing*. But, as I had said previously I *knew* the *truth* about my situation and *understood* how that could possibly affect my life. I learned to *accept* the fact that I would probably live alone but since I have *accepted* that, there came a certain degree of *contentment* with it. The doubts and worries about having that "special someone" in my life were things that were keeping me from being happy, or at least *as happy as I could be*. And for me that was *fine*, I was good with it. However, I didn't *like* it...but I had to *accept* it as what *my* "reality" was like...

As long as I stay true to myself, to the person I *knew* I was, I would be fine. I *cannot* and *will not* allow negative thoughts and feelings control my life.

Crossroads came upon me at times rather quickly, other times...snuck up on me! And each path I chose seemed up to lead me to the same place every time...straight to who I am! What I have just been through and spending over four and a half years recovering from has just confirmed what I have strived for were always there. I couldn't let cancer, the side effects and damage caused...and even the mean shallow people, that sadly, are still out there hold me back or to hurt me OR prevent me from being *who I know I am!*

I've always strived to be the man I *like to think* I am today. That's not meant to seem arrogant...rather...I see it as the only way I can leave a good legacy. It is funny, how I am seeing yet another *good thing* to come from cancer?

*Life is good...yup, it is!* ☺

During the writing of this book, remembering the events I experienced during my "battle" with cancer was very hard emotionally...re-living it all over again. I found myself and an impasse towards the end of chapters 8-9. I had an "detailed outline" of what I wanted to write and how I wanted to write...chapters 8-9 posed a "wall"!

With the events towards the end of chapter 10 will give you an insight as to *why* that chapter is *important*. My hope, is that *you*, the *reader*, can see that the most *unimaginable* situations, both good and very bad...*are with us all* at one time or another in our lives. Having these *specific* "events" were what I experienced in my life before, during and after cancer.

What you are about to read in the next chapter may seem "unbelievable" and some even "unimaginable"...but they *did happen*. And they had several 'effects' on me.

Any cancer patient/survivor can probably tell you...life's situations" of day-to-day lives are indeed *forever changed after cancer diagnosis*.

# Chapter 10

# A *Good* Life and

# *Better* Future

Self Portrait by Kevin K Irish 2013

During the third year of "remission" I continued to live life and enjoy life to the best of my abilities. I'm still able to go on weekends and take care of my family and be there for them if and when they need me. I was also golfing on a more regular basis and actually *improving* a bit. I had taken a lesson from the golf pro at the golf course I like to consider my "home course" and that lesson helped so much, I actually dropped seven strokes from my handicap! This...is a *very* good thing! ☺

Life's gotten better and better and I was feeling better every day. I have been eating healthy and taking my vitamins and supplements all along and truly believe that these have been helping me stay cancer free. And, I have been *losing weight* on a consistent basis! To *me* this was *amazing* as I thought I would *never* get rid of this *lard*. It was so nice to be able to start wearing clothes that fit me better and that I felt comfortable. It was getting easier to get out of bed, I had more energy to do things that I had before and enjoyed going out visiting with friends more often because I didn't feel as *self-conscious* about being *overweight* as I once had. (Overweight? I was *hugh*!) ☺

On my third year checkup with my oncologist, he was unable to check with me that day due to an emergency with another patient. His PA, physician's assistant, filled in for him and we discussed my progress to date. She is an extremely likable and personable person and yet still had such a high level of professionalism that you couldn't help but be impressed by her. She discussed my latest X-ray's and blood tests and commented on how *excellent* everything looked. We discussed my alternative methods and she was very quick to agree and was surprised to find out that there were two supplements that I had taken that not many people know about.

She also commented on how she admired my "upbeat attitude" and complemented me for the weight loss so far. I was feeling pretty good about this time and then we started to discuss those odds once again. When I mentioned the "1 in 3 odds of recurrence" that I was given at the end of my treatments at the end of 2009, she laughed and made the same comment as my Oncologist that the *further* away you get from the cancer and the treatments, the better my odds would get for *non-recurrence*. I should mention that she had discussed my test results and progress notes to date with my oncologist and she informed me that they *both* agreed that my odds of recurrence now were *1 in 5*! (the closer I get to '5 year mark' and beyond...my 'odds' improve to that of someone who never had cancer-although I will never be 'cured'...it's all very good, yeah?) ☺ *I couldn't believe my ears*! This was absolutely *unexpected* an *incredible* news!

She then also informed me that my Oncologist didn't want to see me in his office for another *six months*, meaning that he had such *confidence in my recovery* that he didn't feel it *necessary* for me to have to come in any more than twice a year. *Twice a year? Awesome!* ☺


And...*I have lost over 25 pounds by my 2 year mark and another 15 pounds by my 3 year check-up!* ☺


We chatted a little bit about this and that and at the end of my visit there, she gave me a hug and told me how happy she was and my Oncologist as well, that my progress is so good! She commented to me that the staff there always enjoyed when I came in for follow-ups during the last three years because of my positive attitude and that it seemed when a patient is coming out from an exam, and they seem upbeat and *relaxed* and *feeling good about life*, from a fellow cancer patient, that it seems to "rub off a little" on patients waiting to be seen. This is a *good* thing, as I can *totally* relate to patients who are either just about to begin or have already begun chemotherapy, the *fear* that they are going through. I like to think that these patients, seeing another patient doing well would *encourage* them and *comfort* them that perhaps their outcome would be as good. And I have to admit that while I was going to treatment, when I saw another patient who was doing really good, it encouraged me to forge ahead and complete treatment so I can share in their success. I wanted to be a success story too! ☺

*And it would appear I have succeeded! Yay me! ☺*

As I said earlier, writing this book was *initially* considered by myself to just be a "hobby" or "something to do"...

Passing the three-year mark, I truly feel I have accomplished what I initially *didn't* think I could. The chemo, the radiation, the surgery, followed by even *more* chemo was something that simply surprised me every day that I actually woke up after treatment!

During my research I had found many reports that were *very* discouraging for chemotherapy patients. There were a few coroners reports that stated quite succinctly that 80% of cancer patients who *die* do *not* die from the cancer! They die because of the *chemotherapy*. Going through that crap *twice* verified those statistics as I could truly feel to what those man-made, synthetic and toxic drugs can do to the human body, more specifically, *my* body. No damn wonder people were dying from it!

All during the past three years I have talked to a lot of cancer patients and survivors and found that there is an unspoken *understanding* and *acceptance* between patients and survivors. Again, as each cancer diagnosis is *different* and *unique* to each person common factor amongst all of us is the *emotional damage* caused by the diagnosis, the treatments and the *fear*. If you can see into the eyes of a patient when they realize *someone else* has gone through, or is going through the *same thing as they are*, it's a look of *relief* and *understanding*.

Patients and survivors share another common issue and that is not being able to relate their thoughts or feelings and their experiences to non-patients and survivor's. People ofttimes say that they can *understand*, when in fact, there is no possible way for them to understand unless they receive a cancer diagnosis themselves! When a patient/survivor meets and talks with another patient/survivor the communication is open, honest, caring and heartfelt. The understanding and compassion that is shared between patients and survivors is similar to how World War II veterans, or any war veterans, who haven't seen each other in several or many years, share the same understanding and compassion because they have lived through and experienced, horrific and deadly combat situations with each other. A "brotherhood" if you will.

Surviving *any* cancer diagnosis and subsequent treatments changes one's life *forever*. How that change is made is entirely up to each patient. Sure, there are the physical changes that usually occur, but it's the *emotional* changes that define us as the person and who we are *after* cancer. Whether the diagnosis is at such an early stage or at a later or more advanced stage isn't too important. When a person hears the word "cancer" and their name in the same sentence, you are *never* the same. From the diagnosis, to the treatment and beyond, *will* in fact, change your outlook in life... *permanently*.

I had never have thought of myself as above average or below average, rather I felt I was safely somewhere in the middle of average. I mean, the person I was prior to my diagnosis was the same person that I am today. The positive that came out of my having cancer, was that it *reinforced* my *resolve* to stay true to the person I always *knew* I was and I wasn't going to allow cancer to change that. If anything, cancer and the treatments and the aftereffects merely *increased* my values in myself and enhanced my views on life and inspired me to want to do more for those who cannot do for themselves.

When I talk to other patients I *always* try to *encourage* them to be *strong*, stay positive and to fight like hell! *Never* give up! The same way that I was *encouraged* while I was going through treatments is what I try to do for patients currently in treatment. Like I said hope is perhaps one of the best things in life. If my story, and my outlook on life, can help just one patient, that *every effort* made for that patient is *totally* worth it. A positive outlook is not only just good for battling cancer. A positive outlook is what helps us see our lives more clearly and enables us to *move forward* in our lives in a *positive direction*. Remember...it doesn't matter if you move forward at a "snails pace" or at "warp" speed...as long as you *move forward* (not standing still or going backwards) in your life, your life *will* get better! I recommend going slow though...so you don't miss *all* the *good*! ☺

It's not just a "catchphrase" or something that everybody says but don't practice in their own lives.

Being *positive* and having *hope* comes from your *heart* and from your *soul*. It's an integral part of our lives that can affect *others* as well as *ourselves*. When we project a positive outlook and a positive direction in our lives, it serves as an example to others. ☺

You don't have to walk around with a T-shirt or big sign that says "think positive". There are so many ways to show the positives and good in life by the most simplest of actions. At a store, hold the door open for total stranger. Help a neighbor. Be there for your family and friends and loved ones. It can be as simple as saying "please" and "thank you". Give a smile to someone who's obviously having a bad day.

Make someone laugh. Give someone a hug. *Get the idea?* ☺

About a year ago, during the summer, I was at a party store buying some iced tea. In front of me there was little boy about eight or nine years old. He had an ice cream and a couple candy bars and the cashier rang up his order and gave him his total. The little guy went into his pockets and was pulling out lots of nickels dimes and pennies, dumping them on the counter along with a couple rocks and some pocket lint. As he was counting his change I could see that it was clear he didn't have enough for his ice cream and candy bars. So I gave the cashier a "wink" and told him that it looked like the little guy had enough money for his goodies. With that the cashier acknowledged my wink with a smile and told the little boy that he was all set. He looked puzzled but at the same time he looked happy because now he was going to go stuff himself with ice cream and candy bars and probably ruin his dinner! *Perfect!* That's *exactly* what a little boy *does* with his nickels and dimes, yes? ☺

When the cashier rang up my order I told him to add the difference from that little boys items to mine, and that I would pay the 30 or 40 cents the little fellow was short. I don't think the little boy knew what just happened, but, that wasn't the point. The *point* is that such a *small gesture* as paying a few cents could make a little boy be happy, is *totally worth it*. And, it showed a *positive* effort, even though it seemed so very slight, but it made a difference to three people's lives. First was for the little boy, it was a simple thing, but made that little boys day! Second, was the cashier, because he obviously saw what I was doing and since I was including him to make that little boy smile, was *totally worth it for him*. And for myself as well because I was *able* to make two people feel good, such a small effort as pitching in the little change. Besides, it made me feel good to be able to make *someone else feel good*, mainly the little boy, but it was an added bonus for *me* when the cashier smiled and *enjoy the moment* as much as I did! The cashier told me "God will remember that!" as I walked out of the store. ☺

I feel, isn't this the way it's *supposed* to be? Isn't this the way it *should* be? I say <u>hell</u> yes. Any effort to bring just a *little* happiness or joy or understanding to someone's life, no matter how big or how small, *is well worth it*. And yes you could say that I *do* have a motive behind my actions to help others and to make people smile... My motive is simply this: it makes *me* happy and content with who I am to be able to give *someone* a smile. And if anyone considers this to be a *selfish* act, then so be it. But that's just my opinion.

And I feel that if you put *good* out, for the most part, you'll get good back. It's a *karma* kind of thing. ☺

*Don't <u>expect</u> it though…it <u>will</u> happen…you must have <u>faith</u> and <u>believe</u> it <u>will</u> be!*

This brings me to a few weeks after my three-year remission anniversary.

Around this time, my dad and brother were having some serious health issues *both* at the same time. When I arrived at my dad's home to see how my brother and dad were doing and to do whatever they needed help with, I met a *woman*, who just so happened to tell me she was a "5 year bone cancer survivor"!!! She is a neighbor of my dad and brothers and came over to introduce herself and to chat. Over the next several weeks, as I would come out two or three times a week to take care of my dad and my brother, she would *always* come over to talk with me. We quickly became friends and as time passed, I kept looking forward to seeing her more and *more*. It seemed to me that I had *finally* met someone who *really understood* and could truly relate to what I've been through! We would text and chat during this time and our communication increased even further. After about three months or so, it seemed that we were getting *closer as friends*, and that our friendship was developing into *something more*. I *still* didn't see *anything* more than a "close friendship" coming on. ☺

As time went on, this young lady, who was is also an *incredible mom* would call *me* and tell me when she's going through some rough times. She felt discouraged, alone and unloved. So being the friend and man that I am *and* the *artist* that I am, I was wondering what I could do to cheer her up, and let her know that she was not alone and that *somebody* cared.

Yeah, that *somebody* was *me*, and I *cared*. I would *always listen* and offer encouragement, advise, compassion and understanding, but I also wanted to do *something more*...something *special*...so, I decided to draw her portrait. (it's just me I guess...if someone is unhappy, I like to do what I can to change that, y'know?) As I was drawing, I was able to look into her eyes and see her expression as I studied each part of her face as I drew...her eyes, her nose, her smile, that tiniest lil wrinkle between her eyebrows...

I was really enjoying drawing this "masterpiece"...*this* was going to be a *pretty good portrait*, perhaps one of my *best*.

I was about halfway finished when I had the sudden *realization...* that I had *some serious feelings for her! ...100% of course!* ☺ *Not "in love", per se, but more like a strong "caring affection"...*

*I <u>never</u> saw this coming! REALLY!*

As I knew, *or at least suspected*, that she *may* have *started* to have feelings for me as well, I was surprised when I *realized how I truly felt about her. I simply just never expected it.* It had been over 6 years since I've "dated"...so I had to take this cautiously! This didn't seem real! As nice as it all was...there was something about it...but I was feeling good about life...someone seemed to "like" me for ME...why not?

I was *nervous* and *excited* to see her one day when I went out to my dad's; I had her portrait *with* me.

I'd given her some *little hints* that I had a *special surprise* for her and I couldn't wait to see her reaction when she got that little surprise! We sat on my dad's porch for a while and chatted and not too long after that, I decided to give her the portrait. *The look on her face was of sheer surprise and amazement. IT WAS AWESOME!* Her *beautiful blue's* started to tear up a *little* as she *examined* the portrait, looking at all the little details and nuances that I had put into it.

I told her that I drew her portrait because I wanted her to *know* that I *cared*.

*I just wanted her to smile.* ☺

I needed to cheer her up somehow and feel *better about life! It came straight from my heart.* (I didn't tell her how I felt about her while I was drawing the portrait until *much* later.) She looked me in the eyes and told me that "no one had ever *cared enough* about *her* and how *she* was feeling to do something like *this*!" She gave me a hug before she had to leave. I think she liked it! ☺

A short time after that, we were able to spend some time together...and we went to Wal-Mart's! *It was so much fun!* While driving her back to her home, she wanted me to listen to a song..."One and Only" by Adele. You should have seen the most *amazing* and *loving look* in her beautiful blues when she told me that song was for *me*! ☺

*We had been getting closer every day since...and it feels good!* ☺

Now again...I was not "in love" with her...but it sure was nice to be around her and spend time with her...and I cared how *she* was feeling too. Yup, I liked her alright!

My friends and neighbors comment on how they have never seen me this happy! Now remember, I *never* expected the feelings that I have for her to *ever* happen in the *first place. They* just *did. KARMA* is funny like that, yes? I mean, like I said, I *never* expected to meet *anyone*...and I had stopped looking. Amie felt the same way...she *never* expected or planned on meeting *anyone*...meeting *me*! We *weren't* looking, *didn't* expect it...but it *did* happen!

*However...I was in for yet ANOTHER hurt and disappointment...*

The "wonderful woman" I *thought* I had met...was actually just "playing" me...taking advantage of my "attention and affection" and my good intentions...*with LIES from the day we first met!*

When we first met (when I was going to help my dad and brother when they were both injured), the first day I went to my dads, she came across the street and introduced herself...and that she was a "5 year bone cancer survivor" and was "flirting" from the start...and *that* had made an impact on me! I mean...after everything I had went through and I was *still* just over 3 years "recovering" I had thought to myself; "Self? Only *another cancer patient/survivor* could *ever* be interested in *me*! They could truly *understand* and maybe *accept* me for ME (after cancer)! You have read how things went after that...

I thought she HAD to be the answer to a prayer...

*Nothing could have been further from the truth...*

As time passed, I would do whatever I could to help her and her son (actually *too* numerous to list) but my intentions were good as I understood she was having "difficult times" and didn't want to get me involved. I still cared and just wanted to help if/when I could.

Around mid-March of 2013, she had texted me saying she thought "her cancer was back, stage 3 and she would have to leave state for treatment..."!

I was *shocked*...to say the least! Since she had said she was tired and was going to bed, I didn't call or text back. I let her rest. But I was VERY concerned...and I reached out to her mother...I texted her simply stating if there was anything I could do to help, just let me know. Her mom texted back asking "what are you talking about?" she then called me...and told me that her daughter *never had cancer* and "she tried this *3 times before!*" ARE YOU SERIOUS????

I was numb all over...thinking HOW COULD *ANYBODY* LIE ABOUT HAVING SURVIVED CANCER...AND...SAYING THIS TO AN ACTUAL CANCER PATIENT/SURVIVOR????

That's just plain *cruel* and *cold*!

Her mother talked with me for a while...where we discussed the "troubles" her daughter was having...and that she *knew* I was a cancer patient/survivor (she also thought it was nice that I was helping her daughter).

She said she read (a copy of the manuscript) of this book and felt that I "...was a *good* man." She further said "I appreciate everything you have done for my daughter and grandson"...she even said her "grandson 'adored me'...and that I should "hang in there"...

I was completely shocked and *hurt.* Anger was briefly coming on, but I don't have time in my life for 'anger' or 'hate'. But this *particular hurt* seemed so intentional, cold and *cruel!*

The *trust* was instantly *gone.* It was, though, just the 'grand finale' I guess. After so many "I'll call you" or "I made something very special for you", etc., that never came...ignored or forgotten on birthdays and holidays...I had *enough.*

I felt this was *quite cruel and shallow.* I couldn't believe that *anyone* could be so cold.

I cut all contact with her...and after many attempts to contact me...I simply couldn't trust any words she said.

I do not wish anything bad on her as I always say "the best 'revenge' is by living a better life than those who hurt you". I wish her and her son and family only health, happiness and peace. And at this writing, I think I deserve a lil bit of the same, yeah?

*"The regrets we have in life come from chances or risks we never take."* That's an ancient Greek philosophy, though can't recall from who, but it is so *true.* Well, I learned a hard lesson, but I have no regrets as *my actions were always from the heart.* And that's not a bad thing I think! ☺

But through the hurt and disappointments caused by someone, or through any other "bad" that happens...I seeked out as much GOOD and I could find to replace the BAD I just experienced. A few kind people crossed my path...and I began painting (portraits/acrylic on canvas) and was able to focus the hurt I was feeling into something positive that would make others smile!

To help me through the many disappointments and hurt filled days...I had to do SOMETHING to turn the *hurt* into something *good*...so this is what I did next...

Since I am considered to have *"artistic talent"* and *"skills" I started to paint...*

*...no, not walls...artsy stuff!* ☺

Now mind you, I haven't picked up and "put brush to canvas" in over 30 years...but it would seem that my "artistic skills" haven't left me! I found myself painting like a crazy person! The first painting took me about two months...just couldn't leave it alone kind of thing...

The next painting took only TWO weeks...and it was *better than I could have thought I could do*! *Really*! Then...out of sheer "what the heck" attitude...I decided to paint something I have NEVER painted before...A SELF PORTRAIT! (on back cover!)...it took me nine days to complete! HOLEY SOCKS! *REALLY*? ☺

The *next 10 paintings* went so smoooth! I'm down to just *seven days or so now per portrait*...and they are ALL turning out *amazing* to ME! And I painted them! WOW! ...trying to be a lil humble here...I just find it hard to believe I am painting at this level and, in my view, the *quality*!

All of the paintings were gifts for some special people. I gave my dad the 'self portrait' (which he loved!) and I painted my dad as well for my brother, just to name a couple...

With the "subject matter" (the person in the portrait) with each painting (except my "selfie" painting), the specific photo that I used had to have a certain "feel" to it...a "something about the pose, the lighting...) *compelled* me to paint...and put the recipient at the heart of each portrait. Sound silly maybe, but again, it's an "artsy" thing! ☺

But those "artsy" feelings I got with each photo I used, seemed to just draw out any "artistic skills or experience"...and it just literally flowed through my eyes and through my mind and came out with the gestures of my hands holding a brush. Mixing each specific *color* and *shade* to achieve the desired effect. See? It was a flowin alright! ☺

And yes...the whole experience of being taken advantage of and the hurt involved was very disheartening...very sad.

Then, somehow, and I REALLY cannot explain it, this *urge* to paint and to see if I can make a nice difference in others lives, both with paintings and thru my charity "Kev's Kause"...talking with other patients/survivors...is so very fulfilling...to a point.

See? Replacing the *bad* in life with *good* isn't as hard as it may seem! *I had no idea of what was to come...*

The local paper (St Clair Shores Sentinel) did an article about me and my book, kind of a "local man beats cancer and writes book" thing...it was nice...but still didn't think the book would go too far.

About a week after the article ran, a local resource center for cancer patients and survivors contacted me...ME? Yup...they contacted me to be their "Key Note Speaker" at their "2$^{nd}$ annual Survivorship Event"! ME? A "key note speaker"????

Of COURSE I would...what an honor! So, on June 4$^{th}$, 2013, I gave my very first key note speech!

I was SO nervous that night...and there were A LOT more people that attended then I (or the organizers) expected! (I was told it was the "second largest attendance in the over two years of the center being open!") WOW! ☺

I must also say...what a *wonderful group of people* I had the *privilege* to talk with...current cancer patients (some of the 'newly diagnosed' I was able to sit and try to help), cancer survivors, families, friends and caregivers...and of course, the kind staff at the resource facility!

It was such a *wonderful* experience and so openly received by all there. I even did a lil "Q&A" after...it was fun and everybody participated with such *enthusiasm*! ☺

You can view my speech on YouTube:
www.youtube.com/watch?v=e3sj3WhMKgQ


*It seems to me...that somehow...my book...my story IS making a difference! Maybe it will help others!*

With the TOTALLY unexpected 'success' of my speech and book...I thought to myself: "Self! Let's kick this up a notch!" so, that's *exactly* what I did!

I began thinking *how* could I do *more*...how can I help more patients and survivors?

Since I am an avid amateur golfer...why not start an annual golf outing/benefit? With that, I created "Kev's Kause" (a registered non-profit) and began to organize a golf event! PERFECT!

So began the daunting task of organizing a charity golf outing! ARE YOU KIDDIN ME? ...but I pushed on...I had the perfect golf course on board, giving me a generous "package deal" for the event, furnished prizes at 'cost' and were totally supportive for the event and to help "Kev's Kause"! Now I need "hole sponsors" (to pay for the "prizes") and GOLFERS to sign up and, with their 'entry fee', help fund the event itself (that's how it works!) AND...find additional sponsors who would be interested in donating services or products (for raffle and other prizes)...WHEW! THIS was not going to be easy...and I'm just one person!

I was able to get my local paper to run a small "community event" article...and Fox 2 News Detroit did a story on their website (sadly, it didn't make it 'on the air')...

But with all my efforts...I couldn't get enough "hole sponsors" or golfers to be able to have the benefit golf outing. I was really feeling like I failed...

*But I was NOT going to give up!* ☺

I have already outlined my *plan of attack* for putting another benefit golf outing for the coming golf season...this time...I need to start early...and *remember* what I *learned* from my last attempt!

And yes, during all of this...I golfed as much as I could, painted, and helped other patients...see? ☺

I'm thinking this is a *good thing*, yeah? Besides...I just so happen to get my kicks making people smile! "Kindness is its own reward..." making someone smile on the inside...*PRICELESS!* ☺

The reason I'm sharing this story is because I feel it shows the *power of positive thinking* and the *positive results* even after such a hurtful time in my life *enabled me* to turn the hurt into something *good*...and who knows? Maybe *share* some of that *good*, yeah? So, I have been creating my paintings for friends and family as gifts. And, to help my charity "Kev's Kause", I am attempting to sell my art and put 25% of proceeds into my charity.

See? Taking "bad" and replacing with "good"...and why not spread the "good" around, yeah?

(Did I mention that $5 per book sold goes directly to "Kev's Kause" too?) ☺

By just *living* and *thinking* and *doing positive* in your life...and perhaps doing a little positive for *others*...the results can *amaze* you! The 'results' may be big or small...but any size *good* you *receive* and *find* in your life is AWESOME, yeah?

The woman I just wrote of earlier put a real *hurt* on me...without conscience or remorse...but I do not hold hate or anger, rather hurt that someone could be that cold...*to anyone!*

But I simply *refuse* to let the *shallow* and *hurtful* people in life change *who I am*! I *refuse* to let the "bad" in life change *who I am*! ☺

And the same as when I was going through the chemo/radiation/surgery/chemo...as unimaginable as it all was...I refused to let that change me! It damaged my body...forever changed my life in ways I know...and in ways I fear may be yet to come...*but it didn't damage <u>me</u>!* ☺

I simply remained true to who I am, remained true to the *man I am*. I like to think that if there was any "good" that I may have made in anyone's life that

KARMA was coming along and working its magic! That "positive" thing I keep talking about DOES WORK!

*It always feels nice when you're right about something, yeah?* ☺

Part of my "amateur philosopher" belief is a phrase I created many years ago as a "base" for my own personal outlook/philosophy on life, which says: "What kind of man would I be if I ...?"...*then fill in the rest!*

Simply put, "What kind of man would I be if I" ...*am kind to others?*

"What kind of man would I be if I"...*left a restaurant and didn't pay the bill?*

You get the idea. ☺

(NOT that I would *ever* do the *latter*...I was just trying to *clarify* the *question*, show the *logic* in the *meaning*.)

I have found that this question serves me quite well! It helps keep me *focused* on *who I am* and helps remind me to be the person I *know* I am.

*It's such a simple phrase too.*

As I mention in my first book, when you can *eliminate* as much *negativity* in your life, it's *easier* to focus on everything *good and positive* in your life!

As I have said in my key note speeches...although we are either going through or have gone through the *hell* of cancer and the treatments...there ARE more *positives* all around you!

It seems that we notice and appreciate all the good in the world with a new perspective and appreciation!

Imagine if you will 50 roses and 50 dandelions...in a clear, plastic box. One is a nice fragrant flower, the other a weed. Then, turn on a fan and get them all flying around inside the box, mixing them up in the air! Now, it's more difficult to focus on the roses (good) because all of the dandelions (bad) are mixing up with the roses! When you remove as many of the dandelions (bad) as possible, you can see and focus *more* on the roses (good). *Simple!* ☺

I sincerely hope that after reading how my cancer diagnosis/treatment *effected* me and you can see "how" *positive attitude* and *positive actions helped me*...and I hope they may *inspire* and *encourage* others to focus on the *awesome life they can have*!

YOU are your best advocate! There's no need to bashful! IT'S *YOUR* LIFE!

You are *stronger* than you ever imagined! You have more *courage* than you ever thought possible! But it's TRUE!

YOU SHOULD HAVE FAITH, (*in yourself*)

YOU SHOULD BELIEVE, (*in the positive*)

ACCEPT IN YOUR HEART, (*the good in life*)

THEN YOU *RECEIVE*!

(*Peace and happiness come with it!*)

We can *all* have A Good Life and a Better Future, no matter if you are a cancer patient, a survivor, healthy or not or whatever...by *replacing* the "bad/negative" in your life with as much "good/positive" as you can *see and find all around you*...you can know peace and contentment.

A good friend of mine says: "Cancer does *NOT* have to be a death sentence!"...it's *true*, it's *positive* and *I believe it!*

I say: "Be the best <u>you</u> that YOU can be!"

And...as of the finalization of this revised edition ...I am going to have my next oncologist 6-month check up on April 18, 2014...and it *WILL BE 5 YEARS COMPLETE REMISSION AND STILL CANCER FREE!*

See?

"Miracles are what *seem* impossible...

...*but happen anyway!*"

# FOOTNOTE:

When considering vitamins and supplements for continued good health or therapeutic reasons, ALWAYS consult your family doctor!

The vitamins and supplements I take I have researched thoroughly and am living proof that they do indeed help!

The "all-in-one" multivitamins are ONLY the "minimum daily recommended allowance" as given by the Food and Drug Administration (FDA)!

Regarding marijuana for a *curative* and *preventative* medicine, there are two "types" or "strains" to consider.

The first is called SATIVA which is mostly a THC (tetra hydra cannabin) which affects brain functions and is normally not included for "pain relief or 'curative' in nature, HOWEVER, it has amazing affects for people with certain types of 'emotional conditions'.

The other strain known as INDICA which is rich in CBD (cannabidiol) which has MANY amazing and clinically proven to have MANY *preventative* and CURATIVE effects!

CBD has been proven to CURE CANCER, almost ELIMINATE epilepsy, reduce pain and improve appetite as well as MANY other ailments and diseases!

With over 20 states already havening "medical marijuana laws" the recent "legalization for recreation" is creating a "Pandora's Box" by allowing people to *abuse* this medicinal plant. Marijuana, for ANY reason should NOT be allowed to be available to people under the age of 23 (unless authorized by a reputable physician) and should ONLY be "legalized" for the *exclusive benefits of legitimate patients!*

The fact that people under the age of 23, their brains are still developing! ANY substance that is NOT advised by a doctor can impede the development of the brain leading to problems down the road!

The RESPONSIBLE AND MEDICINAL USE OF MARIJUANA is essential for helping people with *severe* and *life threatening* illnesses and *diseases.*

The "legalization of Marijuana" can *only* lead to BIG PHARMA and BIG BIZ (like tobacco companies) will bastardize marijuana by adding "chemicals, pesticides and .additives' to produce "larger and stronger plants" thus increasing their profits!

I cannot think of anyone who would be willing to ingest by smoking, vaping* or orally consuming marijuana with so many additives and chemicals! How healthy would that be? NO VERY!

*Vaping is using a vaporizer to heat the marijuana with 'convection' heat...no combustion or burning, thus eliminating harmful smoke and carcinogens. By heating without the use of a flame, 100% of active materials in marijuana get into the blood system, more efficiently and a more immediate effect on patients!

# I'm Still Here

## A Cancer Survivors Story

Written and Illustrated by Kevin K Irish

Copyright © 2012

Revised December 2013

All Rights Reserved

## Additional copies are available at:

- Amazon.com

- Barnes & Noble (on line only at this time)

-GoogleBooks.com

- Infinity 520² Partners

- Ingram

-Baker & Taylor

- NACSCORP

-Espresso Book Machine

- And other book stores worldwide
(on line only at this time)

- Directly from the Author

# Original Hand-Painted Portraits

(Acrylics on hand-stretched 100% cotton canvas)

And are available from the Author/Artist, Kevin K Irish.

**25% of proceeds go to "Kev's Kause"**

FOR INFO, PLEASE CONTACT THE AUTHOR AT:

kevskause@hotmail.com

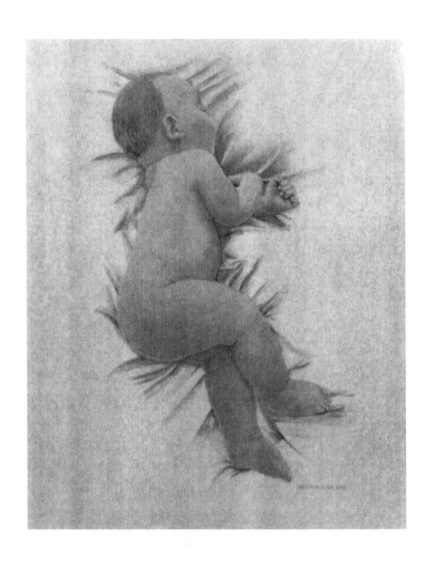

This page intentionally left blank

CPSIA information can be obtained
at www.ICGtesting.com
Printed in the USA
FFOW01n1524221014
8238FF